Total Tripping

From Alaska to Argentina

CARL LAHSER

Order this book online at www.trafford.com
or email orders@trafford.com

Most Trafford titles are also available at major online book retailers.

Printed in the United States of America.

ISBN: 978-1-4907-3746-1 (sc)
ISBN: 978-1-4907-3745-4 (e)

Trafford rev. 05/28/2014

 www.trafford.com

North America & international
toll-free: 1 888 232 4444 (USA & Canada)
fax: 812 355 4082

Contents

Off to see the Glacier

Contents

Introduction

Along about May of 2012, my wife found some deals on cruises. She asked where I would like to go.

Generally, I'm not too thrilled with cruise lines idea of a couple hours shore time and ten times as much of what they refer to as "quality sea time". I thought about this and decided a week would be ok and suggested Cancun, Jamaica, Belize, etc, and found she had booked a trip to see the glaciers in Alaska in August on the Norwegian Jewel. I looked up the weather (60-80°F) and the peak of the iceberg season. Sounds good.

The ship would sail out of Seattle on 11 Aug to Ketchikan, Juneau, the Sawyer glacier, Skagway, Victoria, and returned to Seattle on 18 Aug. We would fly to Seattle and return. There were no good connecting flights to arrive in time to catch the ship on the 11th or fly back on the 18[th.] We booked on Southwest Airlines on Friday the 10th and Sunday the 19th arriving about 2AM on the 20th. Carol booked an overnight in the Best Western near the airport on both layovers.

I had been to Anchorage twice for environmental conferences I had driven out to see the Portage Glacier and down the Kenai Penninsula but my wife had not been along. We had taken the ferry along the Inland Passage from Victoria to Prince Rupert and return. This trip would cover the Alaska Panhandle.

We left the house about 0530, and were in Seattle about noon after a change of planes in Phoenix. (Phoenix had hit a record temperature of 117°F).

Southwest Airlines had changed. They still had cattle car open seating, but they had a new scam—for only $10 you could purchase "advanced priority check-in" to get a lower boarding number. They also loaded in number order. The snacks they served were extremely dry vanilla wafers and peanuts.

The sky was overcast most of the way. Finally, Mt Hood poked into a clear blue sky near Portland. Before long Mt St Helens and Mt Adams appeared and then slid south. Mt Rainier appeared and the clouds dissipated. We landed in Seattle in sunshine.

Mt Rainier

After waiting almost an hour for the hotel shuttle I finally called the hotel. Numerous hotel and rental car shuttles had passed, but I found you had to call and schedule the Best Western bus.

Supper was at the Thai Mango, the self-proclaimed best in the area. It was ok but had a small menu.

Day 1: Boarding time

About noon, we took a shuttle to the ship for $25 per person. It was about 20 miles by interstate and then through Seattle's industrial and port areas.

First boarding activity was picking up room assignments and baggage tags. This was followed by checking baggage. There was an announcement that the bags would be at the room in about three hours so take only what you need for this time period. I set two suitcases down, but Carol wanted her makeup bag with her. I told her she didn't look like she would need any makeup in the next couple hours so she set it down with the other bags.

Then there was a half-hour line for security followed by a half-mile walk to get on board and find our room. Our room was 9166 starboard aft on deck 9. Double bed. Bath. Balcony. Sure beat Navy shipboard quarters.

Port of Seattle

A $12 per person per day ("discretionary service charge") was added to the bill as sort of a mandatory tip. You were encouraged to add more if you wished. There were 1900 crewmembers from 60 countries. All well trained and spoke at least some English. Some also spoke Spanish, Japanese, Chinese, or other languages. There were 1100 passengers from 30 countries.

About 1530, there was a mandatory lifeboat drill. At 1600 they took in all lines and the ship's bow and stern thrusters pushed us gently away from the dock. We were on our way to the Straits of Juan Defuca. We went to supper as we were passing Port Angeles and watched the sun set and the fog roll in as we passed Cape Flattery.

There were a few individual Herring Gulls (<u>Larus</u> <u>argentatus</u>) putting around the harbor and along the channel.

Supper was at the Tsars Palace. Very well decorated. The service and food were outstanding. I won't detail further meals, but they were very good and well served. We ate mostly at the Garden Buffet but tried the Italian and Brazilian specialty restaurants as well.

We moved the clocks back an hour to conform to Alaska Time.

Day 2: Sea Time

The weather at sunrise was clear and 62°. Sea state was 0-4 foot swells. My day's activities included walking around the ship to get acquainted, an Art History lecture and a Park West art auction.

Garden Buffet

The wind had freshened to about 15-20 Kts. This, added to the 20 Kts of the ship, made for a stiff breeze across the deck. The sea was up a little and the water was sloshing out of the pool. The air was cool and wet and salty tasting. Had not seen anything like it in years.

I saw a fork-tailed petrel (<u>Oceanodroma</u> <u>furcata</u>) cruising south just above the waves looking for breakfast.

The Spiniker Lounge was forward on deck 13, overlooking the bow. It was a large lounge/nightclub that could accommodate 150-200. On deck 12 forward was a bridge viewing area, a spa, the library, a card room, and a table tennis area. I tried for the whole cruise to get a tour of the bridge, engineering, and galley, but there were never any openings. I traded in a couple paperbacks for something I had not read, and headed back to the cabin crossing the pool deck and a snack bar.

We went to a variety show at the Stardust and crashed early.

Day 3: Ketchikan

Jet lag was still hanging in there, so I was awake about 0500. It was getting light, but sunrise was still a few minutes off with another hour or so to limp over the coastal mountains. I watched the light intensify, and noticed oil slicks on the surface of an almost flat sea. We were entering the Dixon Entrance about a half hour from Ketchikan, about 1000 miles from Seattle. The tide was ebbing, down about 8 feet. Structures began to appear in along the water's edge including the Tlingit City of Saxman, a First Nation community but not a reservation.

A Coast Guard patrol boat complete with machine gun came roaring out to escort us to the dock between Ketchikan and Gravina Islands inside Tongass National Forest

Ketchikan is called the salmon capitol of the world. It has a population of about 14,000 and has the world's largest population of standing totem poles. About half of the island and a large area of the adjacent mainland are part of the Misty Fjords National Monument.

Totem poles vary in design depending on the tribe and purpose. House poles show the wealth of the family since carving a pole is expensive. Story poles tell folk tales or tribal conflicts. Memorial poles are carved in memory of specific events. Mortuary poles are hollowed out for the ashes or remains of some person. Haida Nation uses symbolic figures like animals and birds or spirits like the wild woman of the woods. Tlingit poles included human figures. There were also shame poles such as the one at Waxman with a figure of Secretary Seward hanging upside down shaming him and the US for a debt not paid to the community. The older poles were not maintained and deteriorated after a few years.

Approaching Ketchikan   Oil slick

Coast Guard   Ketchikan Harbor

Ketchikan   Norwegian Jewel

Occasional Common Terns (<u>Sterna</u> <u>hirundo</u>) and Herring Gulls (<u>Larus</u> <u>argentatus</u>) leisurely patrolled the waterfront.

Air temperature was about 60°. Rain in the Ketchikan was about 400 inches a year and supported a rainforest. This was about twice the Hawaiian rainforest annual precipitation.

After the ship tied up, Carol said her back hurt, and went to the spa. I went ashore and found my tour to the bear rehab center in the rainforest. This was on the south end of the island about 20 miles from the dock.

Ketchikan is an island, and everything comes in by water or air so prices are high. Gas was $4.50. A typical $5.00 burger cost $9.50. There was not much farming since the glacial soil was only a few inches deep.

We drove south to Waxman and stopped to see a Bald Eagle (<u>Haliaeetus</u> <u>leucocephalus</u>). The shame totem pole was still standing beside a rundown building. It was drizzling and foggy so I got no pictures.

Just past Waxman we turned off into the bear sanctuary. We parked and separated into groups for the 2 hour walk. Nursery logs were also bear bridges. Mud had bear tracks. Trees were bear scratching posts. The trees included Aspen and Western Red cedar and Hemlock covered in epiphytes.

Rain Forest

Walking in a rain forest is neat. Cool. Hundred percent humidity. Shady. Quiet. It feels punky under foot like stepping on saw dust. Sound doesn't travel far like screaming in a closet full of clothes. Bear signs. Three inch Banana Slugs in the leaves. Mosses growing on decaying tree trunks. I recognized a lot of the vegetation. Skunk cabbage (<u>Lysichiton americanum</u>). Deerberry (<u>Maianthermum dilitatum</u>). Salmonberry (<u>Rubis spectabilis</u>). Devil's Club (<u>Echinopanax horridum</u>).

The only birds were Common Crows (<u>Corvis branchyrhtnchos</u>) gliding on silent wings and harassing the bears.

While I was crossing a suspension bridge I saw a tan butterfly looked similar to the Hemlock Looper (<u>Lambdina fiscellaria</u>). The guide said she had never seen one.

Zip lines were up in the tree tops. Suspension bridges and observation decks were coupled by elevated walk ways to separate the bears and the people.

Scratching post

Near the end of the trail was a salmon hatchery. Salmon returned to the hatchery where they were stripped of their roe and the eggs fertilized. The fingerlings were released back into the stream programmed by scent to return in several years.

There was a Belted Kingfisher (<u>Megaceryle</u> <u>alcyon</u>) calling and then zipping along the stream.

There is not much animal diversity since this is an island. No grizzly bears or wolves or moose or squirrels. Only black bears.

Bear track, skunk cabbage, salmon berry, fern

Stream

Suspension Bridge

Devil's Club

Momma bear and cubs

Salmon Hatchery

Bear family and deer

Herring Bay Saw mill

At the end of the trail was an open meadow and abandoned sawmill. Four reindeer were penned here. Beyond the sawmill was the office and gift shop. A carver was making a large totem pole. The meadow had Reed Canary Grass (<u>Phalaris arundinacea</u>), Marsh Marigold (<u>Calthra palustris</u>), and tall red Western Dock (<u>Rumex occidentalis</u>). Alder and willow grew along the stream. Western Hemlock trees (<u>Tsuga heterphylla</u>) surrounded the marsh.

Bear clawed boat

A gentle rain replaced the mist of the forest as we headed back to town. We returned in time for a short walk window shopping.

After several shops, I found and bought an elkhorn Billiken. Billikins are similar to a seated Buda. They were first crafted s pop art in 1908 in the US but became an instant pseudo-anthropological item in Alaska saying that First Nation people had carved them for centuries. Its popularity peaked about 1960.

Casting off Lines

About 1500, we began a 600 mile trip to Juneau. We headed NW through Totem Bight into Clarence Strait. Near Arembo Island, there was a starboard turn towards Wrangel Island into Fredrick Sound. Another starboard turn took us into Stephens Passage and the Gastineau Channel to Juneau, the capitol of Alaska.

While in Stephens Passage, I spotted a couple of Orcas broaching in the wake. Not long after this, there were herring leaping out of the water probably running from salmon predators. The ship does not announce such sightings.

Day 4: Juneau

Juneau in the fog

About sunup, fog covered the sea. The world ended just beyond the railing. Soon, land was visibly disconnected from the sea by a layer white clouds.

The ship docked about 0700 with a scheduled four hours shore time available. Most of the tourist oriented shops were open and waiting, but the museum and library did not open until 0900. I had hoped to learn something about my great uncle's trip to the gold rush in 1899. Of the 100,000 that started to the Klondike only about 40,000 actually made it, and only about 4000 actually found gold.

We went ashore, but in the first block Carol said her back was acting up and headed back to the ship. I continued on for a couple blocks looking for the historical museum, library, or a book store. I found that both the library and the museum were not yet open. I stopped in a number of shops and two art galleries before I found Hearthside Books and bought "Native Plants of Southeast Alaska". About 1000 I returned to the ship.

About 1300, we left Juneau for the Tracy Arm Fjord and the Sawyer Glacier. Glacier watching on a cool sunny afternoon! What could be better? Just like I had seen in the Alps, on the Greenland ice cap, and a few spots in the Rockies and the Andes.

Warm sun makes the glacier more dangerous than usual. The ice gets slushy on the glacier's face and meltwater trickles down through the glacier lubricating the base. This increases its speed ever so slightly and causes more calving at the front of the glacier.

The twisting fjord is fed by numerous high waterfalls fed by melting snow fields and tarns backed up by ice dams. Ice flows began to appear. We slowed down to wait for another ship returning downstream.

Tracy Arm Fjord

Ahead, the ice flows were more frequent and larger. Some ice flows were sparkling blue while others were caked in mud. The water became slushy and full of ice flows. The glacier began to come into view around the next bend about a mile ahead when the captain decided the water was too dangerous and turned the ship around. Darn and double darn. That was what I had come for. So much for all the advertising hooey.

Adiabatic winds coming down off the snowfields raked across the deck about 40 mph with a cold chill.

A couple of harbor seals were feeding along the shore, probably hunting for trout, char or grayling.

Snowfield and waterfall

Glacier ahead

Glacier face

Dirty ice

Ice flows

Leaving the fjord

Day 5: Skagway

We sailed up the Lynn Canal and Taiya Inlet to Skagway overnight and docked about 0800. This is the northern end of the Inside Passage. It was cloudy with the temperature in the 60s.

Skagway was a small Tlingit settlement of a few hundred until 1888 when settlers began to arrive. One, Captain William Moore, had a 160 acre homestead and an idea that a shortcut into the Yukon would be important someday. He surveyed the area to Lake Bennett and discovered White Pass. White Pass became an alternate route to the gold field since nearby Chilkoot Pass was more rugged and dangerous. Gold was discovered in 1896, and, by mid 1897, the rush was on. Skagway's population increased to about 30,000. In 1898, the White Pass railroad was started to transport gold prospectors since Canada required each prospector to have a ton of supplies. About 3,000 horses had died hauling supplies over White Pass. After the first wave of prospectors, the country settled into large mining operations, and the railway was settled hauling ore from Lake Bennett. During WWII, the railway carried supplies to the US Army for the building the Alaska Highway. Operations ceased in 1982, but began again in 1988 as an excursion train.

Skagway was the first incorporated town in Alaska. It has a normal population of about 800 that doubles during tourist season. Most of its income comes from tourism and fishing.

Carol took the shuttle into town while I walked the half mile looking at vegetation. Yarrow (<u>Achillea</u> <u>borealis</u>). Dwarf Fireweed (<u>Epilobium</u> <u>latifolium</u>). Dandelion (<u>Taraxicum</u> sp.). Grasses. Seabeach Senicio (<u>Senicio</u> <u>pseudo-arnica</u>). Viscid Oxytrope (<u>Oxytropis</u> <u>viscida</u>). Hairy wild ryegrass (<u>Elymus</u> <u>innovates</u>). Balsam Groundsel (<u>Sinecio</u> <u>pauperculis</u>). Arctic Daisy (<u>Chrysanthemum</u> <u>arcticum</u>). Ornamentals, like mountain ash and lilac were common. Not a bird in sight or sound.

The tide was out, but there was no safe way of getting near the water with fencing and the slick seaweed covered rocks. No shells this trip.

I found Carol shopping and joined her for a couple blocks of jewelry and tourist shops. Two shops had ammonolite jewelry and one of these shops had a couple of large colored ammonites. This pocket of ammonites is located in British Columbia and the nacre is used for jewelry. A local rock shop had some raw ammonolite—not very impressive. They also had lapis in matrix and shrimp fossil from the Wyoming sandstone both of which I resisted. I guess I have finally given up wanting everything.

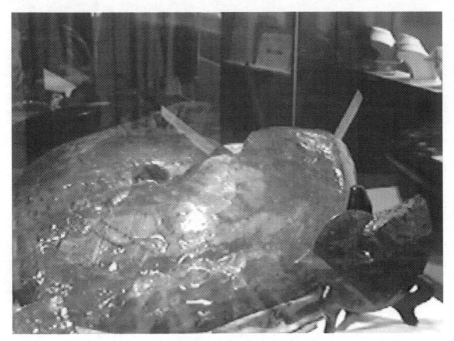

$20,000 Ammonite

We stopped in a Red Onion Saloon to get a Coke since only Pepsi was served on board the ship. The shuttle took us back to the ship for lunch. We had tickets for the train at 1300.

Skagway (originally Skagua in Tlingit) had been a seasonal Tlingit settlement for centuries until the gold rush in 1898 made this a doorway to the gold fields.

About 1300, we joined the line waiting for the White Pass and Yukon Railway train to depart. The railroad was built over two years beginning in 1898 to transport miners over White Pass into the Yukon Territory to Lake Bennett. Our two hour ride would only be about 20 miles to the summit at White Pass and return before we left at 1600 for Victoria.

This narrow gage (36 inch) railroad was chosen as more adaptable to the tight turns and steep grade. The antique passenger cars were pushed or pulled by diesel electric engines. We found our seats on antique flip over benches. Neat.

The train pulled out slowly as the conductor with the conductor hat collected tickets. Past the railway maintenance shops. Past the Gold Rush Cemetery. Along the Skagway River with its sand bars and alder and willow thickets.

We crossed the east fork of the Skagway River fed by the nearby Denver glacier, and did a 180° turn back to Rocky Point with a view of Mt Harding and the Harding glacier. On the other side of the river was the 110 mile hiway to Whitehorse. Remnants of the gold miner's foot and horse trail are still visible along the canyon wall and can still be hiked.

All Aboard

Mr. Bracket built a wagon road up the valley and tried to make it a toll. The miners ignored him and used the road.

Across the river stands Buchanan Rock with large white letters spelling out "On to Alaska with Buchanan". Mr. George Buchanan, a coal merchant from Detroit, established an inspirational camp for young people. About 50 boys and girls were sent to this shirt-and-tie camp each year for about 20 years. The intent was to teach them the art of making money. Some of his graduates painted the sign.

Buchanan Rock

We passed a burial site for two railroaders caught in a blasting accident and saw Bridal Veil Falls cascading down 6,000 feet from glaciers on Mt Cleveland and Mt Clifford.

Heney Station was the site of a freight transfer station where freight was sent down a tram to White Pass City and loaded on pack horses for transport to the summit.

Bridge

We passed along Glacier Gorge across a bridge and into a 1,000 foot tunnel and emerged with a view of Skagway harbor, the Lynn Canal and Mt Harding. We crossed Dead Horse Gulch and bypassed an abandoned steel cantilever bridge that had been replaced by a 675 foot tunnel.

Skagway from Rocky Point

Abandoned bridge

At the summit, we sat on a siding while the engines hooked on what had been the rear of the train. We flipped the seats over and swapped sides of the train to see out the other side. Although we had crossed into Canada we did not need our passports since we never left the train. The border is marked by flags and a mounted police shack.

International Boundary

Skagway River and Mt Harding

No birds. Trees were primarily Mountain Hemlock (<u>Tsuga</u> mertensiana) and Sitka spruce (<u>Picea</u> <u>sitchensis</u>). Shrubs included Sitka Alder (<u>Alnus</u> <u>crispa</u>) and Glandular Birch (<u>Betula</u> <u>glandulosa</u>). Grasses included dry Arctic Bluegrass (<u>Poa</u> <u>artctica)</u> and Glaucous Bluegrass (<u>Poa</u> <u>glauca</u>). Most of the flowering plants were gone, but there were a few False Hellebore (<u>Veratrum</u> <u>viride</u>). Dwarf Fireweed (<u>Epilobium</u> <u>latifolium</u>) was in full bloom. Downtown, between the tracks, grew Meadow Horsetail (<u>Equisetum</u> <u>pretense</u>).

Back on flat land, we got off the train about 1630 and boarded the ship for departure. Destination Victoria, B.C.

Supper was at the Brazilian steak place. For $20 each we got the same or better than we could get in San Antonio for $65 each.

Day 6: At Sea

Not much to do at sea. Read. Walk around. We attended a seminar on Thomas Kincaid, who died a few months previous. He was a good artist, but I never liked the hidden religious symbolism in his later works. He did not like to sell his original pieces, but he made minute changes in each print to make each an original. Another secret is that he saved his hair cuttings and had his DNA extracted and mixed into the ink for the signatures and stamps that go on his prints. One of his early landscapes of Venice offered for sale. It was nice so Carol bought it.

There were clouds in the north, and the sky was broken overcast.

Day 7: Victoria

After docking in Victoria, about 1400 we only had a couple hours to see the town. Carol decided not to go ashore. The museum would close in about two hours so I went for a walk in the residential area near the docks. I had been to Victoria before and this was a new part of town for me.

This was almost a fall afternoon. The houses were well maintained and landscaped. Cute cottages with picturesque flowers.

Back on board, we packed and went to the Tsar's Palace for supper.

Day 8: Seattle and Home

The ship docked early Saturday morning, and people began debarking about 0800. We were scheduled with a group leaving at 1100. Our baggage had pink tags and had been set out the night before. We had a late breakfast and waited for our group to be called. Our plane would not leave for 24 hours. Late Saturday afternoon until noon Sunday.

On the pier, we found our bags and went looking for a shuttle bus to the airport since they would not stop at hotels. The hotel shuttle picked us up at the airport.

Supper was at an outstanding oriental buffet, the Mizuki Buffet in nearby Tukwila. Sushi. Seafood. Oriental dishes. A new dish foe me was deepfried salmon skin. Very good.

Our plane left at 1400 for Reno. After a four hour layover, we left for Las Vegas and finally to San Antonio. We were home O dark thirty Monday morning.

Sidelight-While in Reno Carol stuck $5 in a poker machine, won $10, and quit. Only way.

Comments:

Overall the trip was successful. My complaints were not seeing the Inland Passage and glacier as shown in all the advertising and not getting to see the bridge, engineering, and the galley. I only put on 8 pounds in ten days, but it took three weeks to take the weight off. I would like more shore time and less sea time.

The weather was cooperative. The crew was well trained and friendly. Food was overall very good. The ship was well maintained, and the company had passenger management down to a science.

I can't think of any improvements.

Biologicals

This is a list of plants and animals that I recognized or easily identified. References included:

Field Guide to Western Birds
Field Guide to Alaskan Wildflowers
The Alaskan-Yukon Wild Flowers Guide
Plants of the Western Boreal Forest and Aspen Parkland
Native Plants of Southeast Alaska

Plants

Equisetaceae
Meadow Horsetail (<u>Equisetum</u> <u>pretense</u>)   Skagway

Araceae
Skunk cabbage (<u>Lysichiton</u> <u>americanum</u>)   Ketchikan

Poaceae
Beachgrass (<u>Elymus</u> <u>mollis</u>)   Skagway
Reed Canary Grass (<u>Phalaris</u> <u>arundinacea</u>)   Ketchikan
Arctic Bluegrass (<u>Poa</u> <u>artctica</u>)   White Pass
Bluegrass (<u>Poa</u> <u>glauca</u>)   White Pass

Cupressaceae
Western Red Ceder (<u>Thuja</u> <u>plicata</u>)   Ketchikan

Pinaceae
Sitka Spruce (<u>Picea</u> <u>sitchensis</u>)   White Pass
Mountain Hemlock (<u>Tsuga</u> <u>mertensiana</u>)   White Pass)

Taxaceae

Western Hemlock (Tsuga <u>heterophylla</u>)	Ketchikan, Skagway
Mountain Hemlock (<u>Tsuga</u> <u>mertensiana</u>)	White Pass

Aralaceae

Devil's Club (<u>Echinopanax</u> <u>horridum</u>)	Ketchikan

Asteraceae

Yarrow (<u>Achillea</u> <u>borealis</u>)	Skagway
Dandelion (Taraxicum sp.)	Skagway
Seabeach Senicio (<u>Senicio</u> <u>pseudo-arnica</u>)	Skagway
Balsam or few-flowered Groundsel (<u>Sinecio</u> <u>pauperculis</u>)	Skagway
Arctic Daisy (<u>Chrysanthemum</u> <u>arcticum</u>)	Skagway

Betulaceae

Sitka Alder (<u>Alnus</u> <u>crispa</u>)	White Pass
Glandular Birch (<u>Betula</u> <u>glandulosa</u>)	White Pass

Fabaceae

Alsike Clover (<u>Oxytropis</u> <u>viscida</u>)	Skagway

Liliaceae

Deerberry, False Lily-of-the-valley (<u>Maianthermum</u> <u>dilitatum</u>)	Ketchikan
False Hellebore (<u>Veratrum</u> <u>viridae</u>	White Pass

Onagraceae

Fireweed (<u>Epilobium</u> <u>angustufilium</u>)	Ketchikan
Dwarf Fireweed (<u>Epilobium</u> <u>latifolium</u>)	Skagway, White Pass

Polygonaceae

Western Dock (<u>Rumex</u> <u>occidentalis</u>)	Ketchikan

Ranunculaceae
Marsh Marigold (<u>Calthra</u> <u>palustris</u>)   Ketchikan

Rosaceae
Salmonberry (<u>Rubis</u> <u>spectabilis</u>)   Ketchikan, White Pass

Salicaceae
Aspen (<u>Populus</u> <u>tremuloides</u>)   Ketchikan, Skagway

Insects

Hemlock Looper (<u>Lambdina</u> <u>fiscellaria</u>)   Ketchikan

Birds

Buteonine
Bald Eagle (<u>Haliaeetus</u> <u>leucocephalus</u>)   Ketchikan

Laridae
Herring Gulls (<u>Larus</u> <u>argentatus</u>)   Seattle, Ketchikan
Common Terns (<u>Sterna</u> <u>hirundo</u>)   Ketchikan

Hydrobatidae
Fork-tailed Petrel (<u>Oceanodroma</u> <u>furcata</u>)   Cape Flattery

Alcedinidae
Belted Kingfisher (<u>Megaceryle</u> <u>alcyon</u>)   Ketchikan

Corvidae
Common Crows (<u>Corvis</u> <u>branchyrhtnchos</u>)   Ketchikan

Mammals

Black bear	Ketchikan
Harbor seals	Glacier, Skagway
Orca Killer Whales	Stephens Passage
Mule Deer	Ketchikan

San Francisco
Home Exchange

Contents

Introduction

We received an inquiry about a home exchange in San Francisco that my wife, Carol, immediately accepted. They wanted to come to San Antonio in the 24 March to 14 April 2007 timeframe. I was teaching a class every Monday. We settled on exchanging houses and cars for the week of 27 March to 4 April so I would miss only one class.

Background

I had been to SF a number of times over the past 40 years, and I thought it would be interesting to see another part of San Francisco. I had stayed across the bay in Alameda or in the downtown areas like Russian Hill, Knob Hill, Chinatown, North Beach and Fisherman's Wharf. Over the years, I had seen these parts of town and spent a day seeing Golden Gate Park, another day at Muir Woods and had spent two weeks at the radar site on top of Mount Tamalpais. Never had I seen any of the area south of Market Street or any of the local neighborhoods.

I had spent most of 1959 stationed at NAS Los Alamitos near Long Beach. We had spent the year working and playing surfer, beach partier and would-be beatnik. I discovered surfing, coffeehouses, poets like Ferlinghetti, Ginsberg, and Kerouac, and heard tales of North Beach.

My first trip to SF was actually to Alameda Naval Air Station in 1960. I got to see Chinatown and the view from the Twin Peaks. This was followed by business trips to visit Naval and Air Force civil engineering offices. I also had a two-week AF Reserve assignment to the radar site above Mill Valley that sat atop Mt Tamalpias.

I preferred to stay in the Sam Wong Hotel at 615 Broadway. I liked  it for price but mostly for location where the worlds of Chinatown and North Beach collide. What's more romantic than going out the door into Chinatown for a breakfast of congee in a hole-in-the wall that had tea cups and chopsticks on the table and then catching the cable car to work. Old Sam's grandson now runs the hotel. It was closed for a couple of years for remodeling in the late 90's. It reopened as the SW Hotel. The rate is not $35 a night any more but it's still reasonable. The rooms were small with wardrobe and a bath. There was no AC but AC was not needed. This was a family oriented hotel and along the hall you could hear several oriental languages and smell good cooking.

In 1978 my mother-in-law wanted to go to Hawaii and talked my wife into accompanying her. I arranged a couple of days of business in San Francisco and flew out to see them off. My mother-in-law had reserved a suite at the Francis Drake Hotel for a couple nights. She and Carol shopped and saw the sights while I took care of business. The last evening we had dinner at the Top of the Mark in the Mark Hopkins Hotel. Carol's mother insisted on the place and insisted on paying a $120 bill for supper. They left the next morning. I finished my work and went back home to Colorado Springs. I doubt that we will be eating that high on the hog this trip, but the guidebooks showed even taqueria prices were double San Antonio prices.

Here we go

Our partners in this swap arrived the evening of 27 March. We picked them up at the airport. We showed them our house and then went out for Mexican food and a quick ride around downtown.

We reserved A Yellow cab for 0530 on 28 March. At 0540 I called and was told that we had no reservation, but they would have someone there by 0600. We got to the gate as the plane was finishing boarding. The flight departed late, so we arrived in Houston as our SF flight was finishing boarding. (I found that time between flight legs was 30 minutes for domestic flights instead of an hour.) The next leg of the flight took off 20 minutes late.

The sun came up golden behind rows of blue stratus clouds. Over West Texas we were in clouds until we were over the Sierras. All of the reservoirs were down with little thaw water expected. We flew south of Yosemite National Park and out over the wine country. It was reported to be 51 and clear in SF. We passed over the Coyote Hills Park, the Don Edwards San Francisco Bay National Wildlife Refuge, and the San Mateo Bridge on the way to touchdown near San Bruno. Alameda and San Francisco were visible in the haze in the distance.

Our 3 hour and 20 minute flight to San Francisco International Airport was on the ground just about 11:00 local time. We had our bags about 11:30, and a taxi with a GPS unit zipped us on a $30 ride to our temporary new home with no missed turns (pretty neat gadget). We flew north on 101 past the ballpark and through Daly City and north on Mission Cortland. There was a large, empty farmer's market with murals and graffiti. (There were numerous murals and a lot of graffiti scattered around town).

We put the bags in the house and walked down the hill to find lunch. There was a church to St Kevin on one corner, a coffee shop on another, a primarily beer and wine store on another and a deli/grocery on the fourth. West along the street were Mexican, Italian, American, and Chinese restaurants, a bookstore, an art gallery, several other shops, and a larger grocery. We ate Chinese and picked up a few groceries on the way back home.

We got settled and headed down town. As we waited for the bus there were four black young adults verbally harassing passersby and taking turns on a small bicycle. A longhaired white guy with a plaid shirt on popped into the corner store and emerged with a quart of beer.

The bus arrived to take us to the underground. It wandered down Cortland through Bernal Heights, Noe Valley and the Castro district to Castro and Market. Adult bus fare was $1.50 but we were seniors so it was only fifty cents including transfers. We got off at Market Street and crossed Castro to the Harvey Milk Plaza and Muni station.

We passed several gas stations. Regular was $3.41, mid range was $3.51, and high test was $3.61. When we left San Antonio this morning regular was $2.19.

We rode the MUNI underground rail to the Montgomery Station near the financial district and walked through the almost empty streets to Chinatown. Carol found a Chinese restaurant that suited her for supper. I had salt and pepper shrimp with the shells still on like I like and Carol had a chicken dish. Prices were more than double hometown prices. We were home before dark.

The area around the Castro Street bus stop was interesting. The Castro Theatre showed gay movies. There were several small eateries, a cookie shop called Hot Cookies painted on red briefs, and a bead shop.

When we returned home, I set out the trash. There was a large wheeled container for wet garbage and another for everything burnable that went to make electricity.

The house had three floors and a small backyard. We entered through the garage on the second or street level. The garage had a parked car and lots of bookshelves. We stayed in the apartment that had a kitchen, bath, and bedroom. The bottom floor was filled with bookshelves since our host sold books on-line. The top floor was a more formal living area up narrow stairs. There was a gas heater in the apartment that knocked the edge off the cold. It was in the 40's over night with 50's and 60's during the day. This was a neighborhood of laborers and many of the homes had been owned for years.

Thursday morning we went down to the corner coffee shop for rolls and hot chocolate for $10. We took the MUNI to the Montgomery Station and walked up Sutter. Just past Kearney we stopped at the Asian Art Center. They had some outstanding embroidery pictures that we put a bid on.

Nearby was a modern gallery that was unimpressive. On the next floor was The Square Butte Gallery and John's Western Gallery with some outstanding western art including paintings by Zhiwei Tu of the California Chinese heritage. They had a good collection of art books and a showing of sketches by Joe Brotherton. Brotherton was an artist and dancer. He became prominent later but these sketches were in the Caffe Trieste in the 1950's. (I bought one. Later we visited the Trieste to see if things had changed.)

Down the street was the Sujaro African art gallery. They had masks like some of mine. They also had some outstanding antiques. Maybe I can sell some of my collection.

We stopped at Sam's Grill for lunch. Outstanding. It was established in the 1850's and specialized in seafood. The walls were dark paneling with wildlife prints and mounted fish. Lots of tables but plenty of room. They had some private dining rooms European style that probably dated to the 19 century. I tried their famous Hangtown Fry. This was a three egg and dozen oyster omelet. It was very good but there goes my cholesterol for the week. Carol ordered sautéed liver. The sourdough bread was very good. Creamed spinach was seasoned with nutmeg.

We walked up to the City Lights bookstore. It was still there. They had turned down my book of Southern California transit poetry. We stopped in at the Caffe Trieste and passed the Hungry I and Larry Flint's Hustler Club. The Sam Wong Hotel was around the corner on Broadway. The Transamerica Building was prominent sitting on its four spring-loaded legs.

On Friday morning Carol insisted on driving out to Golden Gate Park and I got to navigate.

Traffic was no problem after she got used to the hills. Once inside the park there was a parking problem. We finally found the parking garage under the museum of science that was closed for remodeling. We learned that the Asian Art Center had been moved downtown. That left lakes, athletic areas, the Japanese Tea Garden, the arboretum, and the de Young Memorial Museum to see.

The de Young Museum has a new facility for what I remembered. It's a new modern structure with a strange looking tower on one end. First stop was the bookstore then the exhibit of 20th century art and aboriginal art. We had lunch in their cafe where I had one of the most artfully served hotdogs I have ever seen. Then we went to the second floor for New Guinea and Oceanic art. We went back down to the first level and took the elevator up to level 9 of the Harmon tower. It had a panoramic overview of the entire tip of the peninsula. Lincoln Park to the northwest contains long closed Fort Miley and Hamilton AFB. The top of the Golden Gate peaked over the top of the Presidio. The major buildings of downtown stood out in the greening spring vegetation.

We left the de Young Museum and went to the Japanese Tea Garden. Azaleas and cherry trees were in bloom. The pagoda and other artifacts of Japanese landscaping were in the Garden. The dragon bridge still crossed the steam so dragons could not cross. A tall Japanese bridge crossed the narrow stream so boats could pass under the bridge.

On the way home we drove home through the Upper and Lower Haights neighborhoods and looked at many of the restored homes. Many of the old Victorian homes had a rounded turret of sorts. There was a legend that the rounded corners on homes deflected bad luck.

Back at the ranch we went out for Italian in Bernal Hgts neighborhood. I had polenta and sausage.

Saturday, we got off the MUNI at the Civic Center Station to go to Union Square. We walked down Market Street through the Tenderloin. There were the older inhabitants sitting along the street smoking and talking and enjoying the sun in front of resident hotels. I remember hearing someone in the Tenderloin district years ago call parking meters homeless outhouses because they held on to the post and crapped in the gutter. Tattoo shops and tattooed people were still there along with young blacks with lots of gold and young blacks that looked half starved. I walked through this area one evening years back coming from a meeting on the Embarcadero.

A group of about twenty young folks were occupying most of the sidewalk in one place. There were only a of couple strip clubs and the porn shops were at least not visible. National hotel chains had opened hotels along the end of Market and were crowding out the former low rent inhabitants.

We turned up Powell to Union Square. The James Flood Building still sits old and gray. This is where the GAP is now located. It survived the 1906 earthquake and was the home of Pinkerton National Detective Agency where the writer, Dashell Hammett, once worked.

A several men wanted to be our guide and direct or lead us wherever we wanted to go for a price. There were a few homeless sitting in corners and at least one stack of bundles where someone had staked his territory.

Union Square is a public park sitting on top of a parking garage. An art show occupied the center. Most interesting exhibits were by a young woman who did oriental themes and incorporating coins and other oriental artifacts into the works (about $400 each) and a young Latino who had some metal sculptures and some things he called shadow figures. They were like wire sculptures but were mounted on a background so that a shadow of the figure could be projected.

From there we went to Gumps. Gumps began as general merchandise store dealing in Chinese imports. It has turned into a high-class department store and was nothing like I remember.

I asked if one of the clerks could recommend a place to eat. His recommendation was Moka about a block away. It was on Maiden Lane next to the Xanadu that was in the only Frank Lloyd Wright building in SF. I had a $9 tuna sandwich and Carol's chicken breast sandwich was even more. I guess I'm still a cheapskate.

We passed a large lady in Maiden Lane who was singing opera for donations. It seemed too cool to me to endanger an operatic voice.

We walked back to the Muni and headed home. We waited for over an hour in a cooling breeze on Castro Street before a full bus arrived followed by another empty bus. The busses apparently have no tight schedule but show up at 20-30 minute intervals.

Sunday morning Carol drove us to the Embarcadero. Nothing was open along Market Street. We drove the length of the Embarcadero and finally arrived at Pier 39. We parked and crossed over to the fisherman's side. This was new since I was in SF last. This area was once full of fishing boats moored to the piers. Big pleasure boats in a modern marina have replaced this. Sightseeing boats and the tours of Alcatraz leave from this area. Boutiques, restaurants and an aquarium have replaced the fish houses.

First stop was the Alcatraz shop where Carol bought a jacket since it was pretty cool. We had breakfast at a place decorated for surfing. Signs were displayed like "the only good suit is a wetsuit" and "dogs and boards must be on a leash at all times". I had a BBQ shrimp omelet.

I heard sea lions barking from the street but did not see them until after breakfast. I remember seeing occasional harbor seals around Alliotos restaurant. Large male California sea lions began to come into the area in the early 1990s. They climbed up on the moored boats and did considerable damage. Tourists were attracted to see the basking animals so the marina was constructed and large floats were constructed and moored to attract the sea lions away from the boats. The sea lions are now one of the biggest attractions in the harbor.

We walked the length of the pier and went to the Aquarium on the Bay. The main attraction is the glass tunnels where the fish swim around the viewers. A tunnel was first successfully used at the lake front aquarium in Chicago in the 1960s.

In the aquarium entrance were displays on specific ecological topics, a discovery room where you got to touch the critters, and a well-stocked bookstore. The aquarium trip began with the fauna under the inner bay piers. The tour proceeds to kelp beds then to fast

water ecosystem under the Golden Gate. Local fish were on view close up along with sponges and other invertebrates of the area. I got some pictures better than any I saw or photographed while diving (So I cheated a little).

We ransomed the car from the garage for $25 and drove across  the Golden Gate Bridge to Sausalito. We drove passed Fort Mason and the Marina Green Park and then along Doyle Drive to US 101. The Golden Gate Bridge is a toll bridge south bound but you get out of town for free. There were a lot of people walking across the bridge.

Sausalito was crowded and finding a parking spot difficult. We finally found a city lot. There were several art galleries including one selling Dr. Seuss prints. We had a pizza then drove back home across the bridge.

Diversadero Street took us south to home. We passed through a variety of neighborhoods. Restored Victorian. Modern. Mixed styles. Art deco. A little landscaping in front like in old Mexico. (Most landscaping was reserved for their backyards). Some were highly restored with six colors and gold leaf. Others were more modestly restored but there was nothing in terrible shape. Median price was over a half million.

Monday morning we walked up hill to Bernal Hill. The hill has a view of much of the Bay area and has a transmitter relay station on its top. Carol stayed at the bottom while I went to the top. I met maybe thirty people running or walking the trails and several exercising their dogs.

There are supposed to be some owls on top of the hill in a grove of pines. It was cool with lows in the 40s and highs in the 60s. Giant Coreopsis was in bloom. Most of flowering vegetation was introduces. The grass was speckled with Seaside Daisies. The only birds I saw were sparrows, starlings and a few gulls in the distance.

Back downtown we got off on Montgomery Station and walked up Sutter to the Asian Art Center. The picture of the Chinese Opera star had sold but they had a similar one for the same price that we bought. We had a good discussion with the sales people. Mr. Sun was from near Chungking and the young lady was from Taiwan.

We stopped at Sam's again for lunch. I had sweetbreads since I seldom saw them on a menu. Definitely had enough cholesterol for the week.

We went to the Asian Art Museum. We began with the bookstore where Carol bought a Chinese style jacket. The elevator took us to the third floor where there were exhibits from China and from south, southeast and west Asia. The second floor had more modern China, Korea, and Japan. Back on the first floor we saw a collection of Japanese baskets.

We walked up Columbus Avenue to see the Caffe Trieste. It changed considerably from the 1950s.

Tuesday morning we went back down town to see more galleries. We first visited the SF Art Academy gallery and the Museum of Modern art. Then we visited about twenty of the galleries located on Geary Street none of which had anything of particular interest. The main store of the Asian Arts Center was on Geary so we stopped there.

Back at the ranch we packed up ready to leave about 0500 Wednesday morning. The taxi arrived on time and we were back at our front door about six in the evening.

Carl

City of Angels

Contents

Introduction

Home exchange number 7 was for ten days in Los Angeles while our counterparts from LA spent Fiesta week in our house here in San Antonio.

In 1959 I spent most of the year stationed at Los Alamitos Naval Air Station near Long Beach with a lot of trips to various parts of Los Angeles. 1978 I attended a conference on the Gray Ghost (as the Queen Mary was known) permanently moored near Long Beach and spent a couple nights aboard the ship. In 1990 I spent a week attending a conference at the Anaheim convention center spending an afternoon at Disneyland and taking a LA sightseeing tour. This trip showed a lot of changes since we stayed in a condo in downtown LA.

Day 1

Six months of e-mails settled arrangements for the swap. We would leave on 17 April 2008 and return on 28 April 2008. We used frequent flier miles for the tickets to Los Angeles International Airport (LAX) and return.

We spent several days cleaning and straightening the house and were on our way to the airport about 0900. Although I had called Continental airlines and confirmed the reservations the plane arrived in Houston with ten minutes to get to the other end of the world for the connecting flight. Of course this was our fault but we got reassigned to the next flight and arrived at the about 1730 Pacific Standard Time.

A taxi for $42 plus airport and gas surcharges totaling about $50 took us to the condo about 20 miles to the north. There were several options for travel to and from the airport other than taxi. One is the Super Shuttle for $18 each. Another is the Flyaway bus that connects with Union Station. Another is the subway service downtown for about $5.00. We decided on a taxi since we really did not know where we were going.

The taxi with a Haitian driver flew down various freeways mostly on the carpool lanes. The hills were visible in smoggy shadows. Palm trees and eucalyptus trees appeared in strings in various parts of town. Islands of tall buildings appeared in a sea of suburbs. Some of the freeways were landscaped with bottlebrush, oleander, Esperanza, and other flowering plants while other stretches were bare or covered with weeds. There was a ¾ moon about an hour up when we arrived just after 1800.

A surprising observation was that probably 90% of the vehicles were black, gray or white. There were almost no tan or brown and very few prismatic colors like red, yellow, green, or blue. During the following week this held and even spilled over into the clothing with only an occasional blue or tan jacket and red T-shirt. I don't remember LA being this pastel. One study says this bland color choice represents maturity.

The temperature was in the lower 50's in the evenings with highs in the 60's for most of the trip requiring a jacket. The end of the week, 24-25 April, had a weather change into the 60-90 degree range.

We stopped at the building security to pick up our key and pass card. There was also a Ralph's discount card on the key ring. The elevator needed the pass card to work.

Our condo unit was on the eleventh floor facing roughly northeast overlooking the tall buildings of downtown. It was about 1000sf with bedroom, bath and kitchen and common area with a balcony located in an area that had once been industrial and hotels. The older buildings were being converted to half million-dollar condos and upscale office space or being demolished. The complex had an outdoor pool, an exercise room, covered parking and security.

There was a Ralph's Superstore across the street. It had groceries and a deli and had expanded into a condo and office spaces to maximize its property. We bought a few necessities. This was a big change from the small, crowded, unfriendly Ralph's that I remember far in the past.

We walked a couple blocks to the Pantry on Figueroa and 9th. The food was home-style and abundant. I thought it was OK but Carol was not greatly impressed.

Day 2

Two hours jet lag meant waking up about 0500 local time and dozing until about 0700. I finally got up and went to Ralph's for milk and a few breakfast things.

I had oatmeal and hot tea on the balcony. It was Friday and the construction work was beginning for the day. Between the construction and the traffic it was noisy. Inside the condo a residual sound sounded like the surf.

About 1000 we walked to 7th and Flower looking for the visitor center. No one seemed to know where it was located. We decided to go to the La Braea tar pit museum. It was officially the George C. Page Museum of Tar Pit Discoveries. Bus fare for us seniors was $0.25 until 5PM when it increased to $0.55. One little booboo was I asked the driver for the La Braea museum and she let us off on La Braea about six blocks short of the museum.

The museum is collocated with the LA County Museum of Art but this is not mentioned in the tourist literature. The fenced tar pit is located just inside the entrance. It is easy to identify with an oily smell, oil sheen on the water and several statues of Mammoths. About ten acres of park contains several statues of saber tooth cats, and other critters from the tar. There were numerous kids resulting in a BE NO park—No bicycling, skating, skateboarding, loud noise or music, etc. The museum proper covered most of an acre with numerous interpretive displays, a bookstore, and a work area. The park is much more than what I remembered or expected. The tour began with an orientation movie followed by wonderful dioramas and exhibits. The bookstore contained several popular books on the exhibits and science along with tourist stuff.

After a stroll beside the tar pit (romantic, huh?) we followed the path to LACMA. It was approaching sunset but the museum was open until 9 PM. We decided we needed more time and would come back on a later date.

Along Wilshire Blvd we found a whole block of little restaurants and chose a Mexican fish place.

After supper the bus took us back to downtown. Old and new buildings. The Miracle Mile. Korea Town. Latinos. Blacks. Koreans. Japanese. Chinese. A few of us none-of-the-above.

Day 3

Saturday morning we set sail for the Huntington Library, Art Collection, and Botanical Gardens located in San Moreno near Pasadena. We tried to follow the signs to the visitor's center but no one seemed to know where it was. We finally found it closed on weekends.

The combination of the Red Line to Union Station and the Gold Line train took us to Pasadena. Two more busses and a half mile walk were still ahead so we too a taxi the museum. It took over two hours from downtown LA to the foothills of the San Gabriel Mountains.

The Huntington estate covers several acres that include botanical gardens, a cactus and succulent garden, a Japanese garden and a formal rose garden. When I was there in 1959 the art collection was in the main house and library. Since then a separate art gallery, the Scott/Euburu gallery, and a huge greenhouse have been built. There is also a collection of Huntington's railway cars that were still running until 1961. I remember seeing "Pinkie" and "Blue Boy" in the main house and taking a quick trip through the gardens. Main house was being renovated. The antique furniture was displayed around the museum.

After the art I went to see the plant collections while Carol rested. The gardens were different than I remember. The greenhouse was new and well designed.

The entrance to the park was lined with plants for the organizational plant sale. Nice specimens but many would not survive in San Antonio not to mention I was a thousand miles from home.

Day 4

Sunday morning was quiet. No Construction. Less traffic. Someone's car alarm went of five times. Temperature was about 70 with a breeze.

About 1000 we left for Chinatown. The red line train took us to Chinatown station on College St. We walked a block over to Broadway, the main street of Chinatown. There were several mall-like shopping areas with numerous small shops. There were few stand-alone shops along the street. There was also the cultural centers and health centers.

New Chinatown used to be much more like a Chinese community when Broadway was a much narrower street and more shops were along the street rather than in malls.

A little after noon we hit the Sam Wu Chinese restaurant that several people had recommended. Tables were set with chopsticks and teacups and the menu was in Chinese with English subtitles. My kind of place.

The place was crowded and the food was good. I saw they had congee on the menu and ordered a bowl to go with my salt and pepper squid. In case you are not familiar with congee it is basically rice soup often with the addition of spicy accents like roast duck or shredded pork. This was the only Chinese restaurant I saw that served congee.

Day 5

We started out to see the world on a beautiful Monday morning. It was cool so Carol decided to stop by Macy's to shop for a jacket.

We found the LA visitor center and got some maps and advice on what to see.

We caught the train to Union Station and walked a block to el Pueblo de Los Angeles and Olvera Street. This historic district was the place where Los Angeles was founded in 1781. There were numerous shops with more Mexican crafts and artifacts than I saw in anyone place in Mexico. I bought a T-shirt with a Pancho Villa picture. We had lunch at a Mexican restaurant.

We took the train one stop to the Civic Center and walked along Broadway and Spring Streets to Pershing Square to catch the subway. The area along Broadway was much as I remembered it. Skid row.

Bird distress and predator calls were being played to scare the pigeons but the pigeons didn't care. The recording probably aggravated the tourists and the homeless that were sleeping in the park a lot more. By the subway ticket machines a young black man was harassing a young Mexican woman who had not figured how to work the ticket machine. He was hollering that that is why everyone should speak English.

Day 6

Tuesday morning we went back to Pershing Square station to visit the jewelry district. There were two blocks of jewelry stores and a couple huge jewelry mall with beaucoup dealers. The prices on jade and colored stones and gold were up but pearl prices were down.

We passed back through Pershing Square to the subway,

LA Pershing Square

Homeless people
Sleeping in the bushes
Pissing on the hero statues
Snoozing in the sun
Homeless.
Hopeless?

We went back to Chinatown to see the Chung King Road galleries. All the galleries were gone or closed.

Lunch in a second Chinese restaurant was a lot less satisfactory. Service was slow and the food only passable.

We walked over to look at the modern Music Center and Walt Disney Concert Hall. Really neat curved steel sheet construction.

Day 7

It was Wednesday and time to see the Getty museum. The trip took two busses. The first bus went along Wilshire to Woodward Ave and the UCLA campus. The second bus passed through the campus and northwest to the museum. Inside the gate was a tram that transported visitors up to the museum on the edge of the Santa Monica Mountains. The views from the tram included much of the LA basin.

Richard Meier designed the outstanding architecture. Massive but airy. The tour began with a short orientation movie. We went through the courtyard with outdoor statues to the Central Garden designed by Robert Irwin. Beautiful. It contained a central water feature surrounded by terraces of color.

Art works includes 17th and 18th century French art and furnishings, illuminatrd manuscripts from the Middle Ages and Renaissance, drawings from the 14th to 19th centuries, photography, European art and sculptures.

After several hours walking we had lunch and took the tram down the hill to the bus stop.

After looking at Macy's and hitting Border's bookstore we went to the Sheraton Hotel dining room for supper. We just are not night people.

Day 8

It was a couple degrees warmer when we headed out to see the Los Angeles County Museum of Art. There was enough of a breeze to keep the smog dissipated.

The bus driver appeared to be frustrated?, bigoted?, angry? Anyway the large black driver stopped the bus so that the door straddled the street sign or other obstruction so customers had to work around the obstruction to board the bus. It's the little things that make some people happy.

The Hammer museum with photos and sketches and the Japanese pavilion were closed for installation of new exhibits. We went to see the modern and contemporary art with a large exhibition of Chicano(?) art. Interesting concepts. Experimental art like ceramic tile. There was one quilt made from T-shirts from Goodwill. Most of the modern art was huge paintings and installations. On the way out we passed an installation of a hundred historic streetlights.

We caught a train out to Universal City Studio. Universal diversified many years ago with studio tours and eventually hotels, a shopping mall and a theme park. We took the tram to the shopping mall and walked through the various shops. W had lunch at a Mexican restaurant and decided not to go to the theme park

Day 9

It was Saturday morning. I sat on the balcony for tea and reading and noted the smoke from the foothills fire. About noon we went to the Museum of Contemporary Art (MOCA). Displays were mostly paintings but there were a number of installations. In the entrance courtyard was an airplane made from crashed airplane pieces.

We followed a list of galleries addresses in the downtown area. Some were out of business and the rest were closed. Walking on to the Pershing Square Station we stopped to look at Angel flight. This was a funicular railroad leading down from residential Bunker Hill Olive Street to the more business-oriented Hill Street. In 1901 it once cost a penny each way. When I rode in 1959 it cost a dime. It was demolished in 1969. A second one was opened in 1996 using the old equipment but was closed in 2001 after a serious accident.

Day 10

Sunday morning was quiet. I read most of the day while Carol went to a mall. We went out for supper to McCormick and Schnick seafood restaurant on the 4th floor of a bank building. No wonder we could not find eateries. We had eaten in this chain in Seattle and Vancouver. Good food and a good desert.

We packed up and I called to make a Super Shuttle reservation for 0500.

Day 11

The shuttle arrived on time for a 30-minute trip to LAX. We both wound up with center seats so I slept all the way to Houston. After a 3-hour layover and a 43-minute flight we were home in San Antonio.

For history of Los Angeles, California, you can browse the internet through Google or Wikipedia.

SUMMER'S END

Southern California

Revisited

Transit Poems

Contents

DEDICATED

To

Lawrence Ferlinghetti, Allen Ginsberg, Jack Kerouac and City Lights Books who introduced me to dynamic poetry in the summer of 1959;

to Beat places that now exist only in memories like Frankenstein's in Laguna Beach, the Prison of Socrates in Newport Beach, Hungry I, the Place and the Party Pad in San Francisco;

and to the California girls and party beaches, still cool but forty years older.

Looking Forward to California

I'm looking forward
to a vacation in Southern California,
from a condo in San Clemente
to see if my California is still there.

I spent a Navy year
in Southern California
in 1958-59.
I wonder what will still be there to see.

September and part of October—
Navy boot camp in San Diego.

October to Christmas—
Naval Station San Diego.
Fleet landing.
Tia Juana.
Trying to get a drink in every bar
on Broadway in a night.
Balboa Park and the zoo.
Point Loma and Scripps Institute.
An earthquake.

New Years to Labor Day
Los Alamitos Naval Air Station
south of Long Beach
and across from the race track.
Anaheim and Disneyland
The Red Car to downtown LA
New Years Eve on Hollywood Blvd.
A lime green '49 Ford convertible
with Von Dutch striping.
Night runs to Hollywood
or to the beaches.
Body surfing on Tin Can Beach.
Beatnik evenings at

Turks in Surfside.
The Prison of Socrates in New Port
Frankenstein's in Laguna

with beatnik poetry of Ginsberg and Ferlinghetti.
Studio tours, Kim Novac, starlets, screenwriters.
Walking guard duty
on the flight line in pea soup fog.
Disney Land for $8
and Knott's Berry Farm for free.
Barry Goldwater's daughter and nieces
surfing at Laguna.
All on the $ 121 a month.

Is my summer over?
The question is not if but changed how,
a quantum leap from the past to now.
15 April 96

San Diego Overview

It had only 570,000 people in 1958. The
    City has grown 300,000 in 36 years
    and the County population doubled.
It used to be a Navy town
    with half a hundred bars along
    Broadway gone with urban renewal.
Fleet landing was where Navy wives
    Could be picked up and be in the sack
    before the liberty boat got
    husbands and lovers to their ships.
    It's a respectable park.
The Coronado ferry is long gone
    replaced with a high curving bridge.
The strong Spanish and Mexican heritage
    has changed into a yuppie and tourist
    Mecca with parking meters and
    entrance fees into our missions.
San Diego has blossomed
    palms, bougainvillea and pelagorium.
    Fire resistant Ice-plant has invaded
    highway right-of-ways and hillsides
    greening the area.
It's still cool and damp
    and fog hangs over Point Loma,
    but the good life I remember is gone,
    gone with numerosity,
    drowned in a sea of people,
    lost in a bevy,
    adrift in a cloud,
    an unorganized hive of vehicles,
    a maze of freeways.
The changeless surf and beach call is weak
    muffled and filtered through
    a fine mesh of bureaucracy,
    parking meters and pollution.

Piers and groins and breakwaters
    stop the sand migration and dump it
    into the unrecoverable depths.
Thermal pollution from power plants,
    freshwater pollution from storm drains,
untreated sewage that gives
    swimmers the itch and crud.
Overregulated vehicle exhaust
    whitens the skies
    and burns the eyes.
It was not perfect 40 years ago, but
    half the people and regulations
    attracted this population
    that is fouling its nest.

La Jolla

A village of 500 Navy and academics
    on Point Loma in 1959
Scripps Institute of Oceanography
    was a single building
    with a few working fish tanks.
I walked a couple miles from the end of the
    bus line to see the stocky director
    with a short, blond flat-top.
Prospect Drive that now rivals Rodeo Dr
    in Hollywood did not exist.
About 30,000 people cover the point and
    encroach on the Torrey Pines.
Scripps Aquarium was replaced in '92
    by the Stephen Birch Aquarium.
    I guess they put your name
    on the place if you donate
    seven million dollars and a hilltop.
The Museum of Contemporary Art was free.
    Graphic and pointless.
    I would have spent the two million
    on other art.
    Money does not always equate to
    taste.

Quail Botanical Gardens

Near Encinitas on 30 acres
    of Ms Larabee's ranch
    sits most of her plant collection.
    Foundation supported and
    maintained by docents
Bamboo, palms, Protea, native plants
    presented well.
A Mediterranean climate supports
    a wide variety of tropical plants

Cinco de Mayo

The celebration of a Mexican revolution
recreation of the violence in a party
The reasons for the war
are largely forgotten
but praise be to any war
that gives us a holiday.
Viva Cerveza!

The Beaches

Rugged beaches along US 101
    are now hidden in state parks
    along the Coast Highway
The water is still cold and
    the currents are bad
The dedicated surfers
    still jump fences to get wet
Surfing vans replaced
    by car top racks for surf boards
    encased in protective covers
No more
    hundred pound 12 foot
    mahogany surf boards
    or balsa boards
    or boogie boards
    or flying saucers.
Light boards of fiberglass with two keels
    and bungee cords around the ankle.
Sure is easier and safer.

San Diego Wild Animal Park

Founders Day

A day with no entrance fee
Three times the normal crowd
including me.

Flamingos

Why stand on one leg Mr. Flamingo?
To save body heat?
How do I know?

Native Village

Beneath a bridge over a waterfall,
Congo fish trap catches nothing at all.

Lowland Gorillas

Gorilla Daddy, Baby and Mom
sitting together under a palm

Bee Eater Birds

An enclosure of Bee Eaters
feathered bright blue and red
with a bee hive in the corner
to keep them fed.

Butterfly Garden

Moths and butterflies
at feeders and flowers,
alighting on fingers
I could watch them for hours

Cat Canyon

Lions and tigers hiding by day
waiting till evening
to come out and play

Kangaroos

Marsupial cousins
mostly Reds and Grays
A Joey still feeds in the pouch
then runs off to play

The Monorail

A two-hour wait for a five-mile ride
seeing strange animals
on a silent glide

The Ride

Zebras, Wildebeest, giraffes and such
endangered species
saved from the clutch

Rhinos

White rhinos aren't white.
Black rhinos aren't black.
But they are both blind and ornery
and social skills lack.

Elephant Moms and Dads

Moms stay in herds with kids and friends
When the kids mature their easy life ends

Dads live alone, solitary lives
I might too if I had 15 wives

Przewalski's Horse

This endangered species
was never rode
and almost extincted
for not toting his load.

The Two-Thumbed Koala

The two-thumbed Koala
is not very quick.
He eats eucalyptus leaves
and never gets sick.

The Reticulated Giraffe

He is 17 feet tall
in his stocking feet
and his tongue adds another foot
to get tree leaves to eat.

Luncheon Monologues

At the Tuto Mare in New Port Beach

White shirt and dark tie, pinstriped jacket
draped over the back of his chair.
    "I play 18 holes at 29 Palms
    before I drive to work every day"

No makeup with a turtleneck and blazer,
    "Did you hear about Jim?
He's HIV but
    he will probably die first from throat
    cancer sucking a nasty cud of tobacco"

Mr. Shades with a pound of gold hanging around his heavy neck
    "Was going to take the boat to
    Ensenada but I got this call from
    Hong Kong . . . ."

Blue silk suit,
    "Well, I never have a cash surplus.
    All the mags say to keep invested"

T-shirt, ear rings, denims and sandals
    "My back is killing me. Our two year
    old still sleeps with us and I didn't
    want to squash him"

Restoration Hardware

A store
with all of Taiwan's gimmicky tools
from the 50's and 60's
to sell to us fools

Tin ware,
Russian magneto flashlights
goose neck lamps
and other nostalgic fancy flights.

MESEMBRYANTHEMUM

California Ice-plant, a fire resistant succulent used to be called

Mesembryanthemum

But a botanist looked at the Fig-Marigolds
and decided this musical name
was no longer valid and changed it to

Cryophytum crystallinum

Pretty but not quite so melodious

Disneyland

Paradox

> I was last here in '59
> when the Matterhorn was a state of mind
> Now I'm back after forty years
> and the Matterhorn is closed for repairs.

STAR TOUR

> Half mile line to board the shuttle
> the robot crew all in a muddle
> Dives and twists into hyperspace
> a light year trip while standing in place.

SUBMARINE

> The sub leaves the tropics
> then under the pole
> the reefscape is neat
> but not quite whole
> shell in unnatural poses and distribution
> and fish in a state of terminal confusion
> Around the world and mermaids too
> in just ten minutes the time just flew.

TOM SAWYERS ISLAND

> Ole Tom's island is hard to beat
> Lots of caves that are really neat
> A fort on the waterfront from olden days
> A suspension bridge
> made some eyes glaze
> A keg bridge where you got your feet wet
> A ride on a flat boat, as good as it gets

Haunted Mansion

The old haunted mansion has lots of demons
that scream in the dark
and the kids kept on screaming
Ghosts and skeletons, spirits and hants
"Let's redo it till Mom says can't"

Jungle Cruise

Hippos, snakes and crocodiles
from the safety of our boat
Tropical plants, fierce natives, and
the captain's
infantile jokes

Enchanted Tiki Room

The only exhibit I had seen before
was the wisecracking Hawaiian birds
They and the monkeys and tiki posts
moved their mouths as they said the words

Crows

Along about sundown
a flock of crows
circled the Matterhorn
cawing, cawing.

San Clemente

Sixty years old and the self-proclaimed surfing capitol of the world.
San Clemente and Oceanside
    mother-in-law
    for Marines at Camp Pendelton
Now, Los Angeles and San Diego
    sleep here only two hours away
    by I-5 or Pacific Coast Highway
Some old money and a lot of new.
Three times the people of 40 years ago.

Ralph's

A friendly local grocery chain
with a sign on the turn stile,
"Check your bags before entering".
At 7 AM all the carts were filled
with goods for stocking shelves.
A daily or shift inventory . . . .
Crooked customers or employees?

Santa Ysabel

Sixteen miles east of Ramona
past winding Highway 78's
rocky canyons and bleak hills
lives a couple hundred people in
Santa Ysabel.
Mission Santa Ysabel, a grocery,
a bakery, a general store and school.
Buffalo T-bone was $18 a pound.
Cider was fresh and cold.

LA News, Thursday May 9

A 71-year-old grandmother held up
    a gas station
    for money to pay back taxes
A city bus hijacked
    and held hostage for two hours
A celebrity goes berserk
    shouting obscenities at traffic
    with a loaded gun in his pocket
A battering husband shoots his wife
    in front of his son
    and is killed by deputies
Weather is smoggy and mild
Pollen is up—Eucalyptus and Avocado

Traffic Signs

I-5 North Use Right Lane
But not at this intersection
where the right lane must turn
and not the next intersection
which goes to I-5 South.
Finally, behind door number three
is the I-5 North ramp.

San Clemente Yards

Small houses on steep hillsides
small steep yards
-     covered with Bird of Paradise
-     hidden in trees
-     planted in prostrate junipers
-     beds of Lily-of-the-Nile in Ice-Plant
-     Torrey pines and Monkey Puzzle trees
Hot dry days with cool damp breezes
Lots of wind but it never freezes

Windmills of Palm Springs

Forty years ago
Signal Hill near Long Beach
was scarred and black
from and with pumping oil wells.

Today a hundred hills sprout
giant white three-bladed windmills
taking energy from the wind and sun

All energy is not the same.

Going to the Desert

Dana Point to Palm Springs

Cool, Moist Ocean Breezes to
Hot, Dry Desert Stillness.

East on Highway 74
past Mission San Juan Capistrano
then 35 miles of climbs and dives
and twists and turns
like a dog-fight on the ground at 25 knots

A motorcycle rally
at a camp ground near Lake Elsinore.
Pairs and small groups
flying low through the hills.

Forty miles of fertile Temecula and
San Jacinto Valleys through Perris and Hemet with dairies, oranges,
alfalfa, strawberries and other truck crops.

Up the Hemet River into the pines
of the San Bernardino National Forest
into the cool Santa Rosa Mountains
almost a mile high

The Reservation of the Santa Anna band
of the Cahuilla Indians leaves the trees
and the cool to wind down switchbacks
to near sea level and the desert.

At Palm Desert with green golf courses and estates hidden behind tall
oleander hedges Hwy 74 dead ends.
A choice of north or south.

To the south is Indio and date production
and the Salton Sea and the Imperial Valley.

We went north through Rancho Mirage and Palm Springs with large, expensive homes, art galleries and trendy shopping.
Mist sprayed to cool the citizens when the temperature was 111 and humidity 10%.
Half the city land leased from the
Aqua Caliente band of the Cahuilla Indians.

A side trip to the Indian Canyons with palms, streams, rock art and casinos.

Then back west on I-10 to Beaumont and Riverside and Perris
to dog fight back to Dana Point.

Laguna Beach

Laguna Beach has changed
from a sleepy retirement village
along the shore and One Oh One
to an artsy yuppie bottleneck
on the Pacific Coast Highway.

The beach I surfed and slept on
is a public park
hidden behind parking meters. Frankenstein's CoffeeHouse is gone
replaced by a motel complex.
Everything is gone with storms,
flash floods, urbanization and time.

My California summer is over.

Leaving California Feeling Good

My vacation is over.
My summer is through.
We all grow up and
there's still plenty to do.

Driving to San Diego
to catch a plane
we passed through Camp Pendelton
where Marine Corps reigns

Off the coast were anchored war ships
for games on the beach
to get them ready to grasp
whatever we ask them to reach.

On the perimeter road along I-5
were three Bradley fighting machines.
The lead one carried the Stars and Stripes
and each had a dozen marines.

I tooted the horn and gave them thumbs up. Each of them carrying full
field pack
shouted "Semper Fi" and saluted
and each of them waved back

ORGASMIC

My Summer is Over

My Autumn is here

Under the Southern Cross
Hidden by Clouds

SOUTH AMERICA

JUNE 1990
MACHU PICCHU, the AMAZON, BUENOS AIRES

Contents

Poem List

Forethoughts

WHERE WOULD I LIKE TO GO

You ask where I would like to go.
Swim in the tropics?
Play in the snow?

I would like to dive Cancun
Study old temples
And walk the beach in the moon

Or go off to the desert
to capture some snakes
And look at the cactus
And walk the dry lakes.

Or look at the flowers
as we walk through a park
Hear rippling water
and the song of the lark.

Or off to the north and the Eskimo
W here the caribou wander
And there's plenty of snow.

I'm peripatetic but you must understand,
I won't go anyplace
I can't hold your hand.

Preparation

In March 1990, we received a small inheritance from Carol's aunt's estate and decided to take a once-in-a-lifetime trip. I suggested Cancun or Baja both with beaches. Carol disagreed. We looked at the Inland Passage to Alaska or a trip down the Mackenzie River in the Northwest

Territories and the Yukon which would follow the footsteps of Uncle Otto's trek to the gold rush in 1898. After looking at brochures and prices and much discussion, we settled on a trip to Machu Picchu and a three day ride down the Amazon. Carol decided that since we would pass through Miami that we should see Disney World. We did our homework, bought a camcorder and extra batteries and got the recommended shots.

Planning and preparation should be fun and a learning experience itself. It should be an important part of any trip. To check out the current political situation in Peru, Colombia, Brazil and Argentina I called the Air Force Office of Special Investigations (AFOSI) and got their anti-terrorism brief. I next checked medical area intelligence reports for the area. These reports consisted of the Disease Vector Ecology Profile (DVEP) prepared by the Defense Pest Management Information Center and the Monthly Disease Occurrence (Worldwide) from the Armed Forces Medical Information Center. I also called the Communicable Disease Center (CDC) Malaria Hotline [(404) 639-1610].

For background information and historical setting, I read or at least browsed through a number of books:

The Amazon by Hakon Mielche (William Hodge & Co, 1949) is about his 1948 trip up the Amazon to Manaus, Brazil.

Vagabonding Down the Andes by Harry A. Frank (Century, 1917) covering his 1917 trip was out of date and did not cover the area of our trip.

Ten Keys to Latin America by Frank Tannenbaum (Vintage Books, 1960), *A History of Latin America* by George Pendle (Penguin Books, 1981) *Social Change in Latin America Today* by the Council on Foreign Relations (Vintage Books, 1960) provided insight into social changes.

Slaver in Paradise, the Peruvian Slave Trade in Polynesia, 1862-1864 by H.E. Maude, *Everyday Life in the Incas* by Anin Kendall (Dorset Press, 1989), *Carnival and Coca Leaf: Some Traditions of the Quecha Ayllu* by Gifford and Hoggarth (Scottish Academic Press, 1976), and *Sicuanga Runa, the Other Side of Development in Amazonian Ecuador*, by Norman Whitten (U. Illinois Press, 1985) provided insight into the development in the Amazon.

The United States and Argentina by Arthur Whitaker (Harvard Press, 1954) covers history and relations with Argentina.

Two travel guides, *The Visitor's Guide to Peru* (Moorland Publishing Co., 1989) and the earlier *Peru Traveler* by Selden Rodman (Meredith Press, 1967) give valuable travel information.

Books on birds consulted included *A Guide to the Birds of Panama* by Robert Ridgley (Princeton Press, 1976), *Guide to the Birds of Venezuela* by Meyer de Schauensee (Princeton, 1977), *The Species of Middle American Birds* by Eisenmans and F. M. Chapman's *My Tropical Air Castle* (1929) and *Life in an Air Castle* (1938).

Plant books were less abundant. I used general references such as Graf's *Exotic Plant Manual, 4th ed.*, and general family keys. I did not have access to Croat's *Flora of Baro Colorado Island* (Stanford, 1978) or Schultes and Raffauf's *The Healing Forest, Medicinal and Toxic Plants of Northwest Amazonia* (Discorides Press, 1990) but probably would not have needed them.

Our travel agent arranged tickets and reservations through Tara Tours for Lima, Machu Picchu, and the Amazon with a side trip to Buenos Aires and a Disney World stopover on the way back.

Passports and our visas for Brazil finally arrived. We were packed and ready to go on the 8th of June, 1990.

* * *

8 June. San Antonio to Lima

Our trip began well. The Checker cab was a few minutes early. The driver said they had two cabs on duty at Ft Sam every morning. United Airline was on time from San Antonio to Dallas-Ft Worth International and from DFW to Miami.

SAN ANTONIO AIRPORT, JUNE 8 1990

We arrive at the terminal
In the predawn dark
It's to DFW and Miami
For a South American lark.

The dimly lit terminal,
Florescent lit gloom,
Feels more like embarking
On a trip to the moon.

An international check in
With passports in hand
Two hours before boarding?
I don't understand.

They check passports and tickets
And hand back a boarding pass.
It's off to the gate to watch
Airport lights through the glass.

*   *   *

In Miami, our run of luck hit a small snag. We had super saver tickets for a United flight connecting with Aeroperu to Lima. Aeroperu had changed its schedule, and United said "You better be ready when we are." United was not responsible for the actions of Aeroperu and would not allow a ticket change. Our travel agent rebooked us on an Eastern Airline flight that left Miami about the time Aeroperu should have departed. This should have been a warning about Pizarro's idiot children's airline.

It sounds simple except the travel agent had not completed her part of the action. After waiting in line for half an hour at the Eastern international gate in Miami, the Eastern clerk told us to go back to Aeroperu. They needed a "fin" or voucher for Aeroperu to pay Eastern which is normally handled by the travel agent. This required a trip to the opposite end of the terminal and an unsatisfying encounter with a bellicose Aeroperu employee. She told me there was no plane to Lima today, and that I "should have caught the plane last night." I resisted the temptation to play the ugly American and finally got my vouchers. This satisfied Eastern Airline's bureaucracy and away we went.

It was a smooth and uneventful flight through the night over the Bahamas, the Windward Passage, and Curacao then across Venezuela and Colombia and half the length of Peru. We arrived in Lima about ten o'clock at night Lima time (eight in the evening by my internal clock).

Lima, from the air, was not exciting. Few lights were visible giving no clue that a large city was present. The airport looked like San Antonio's airport had looked twenty years ago—no jetways and only two concourses. Passengers embarked and offloaded using a ramp hand pushed up to the plane and then walked to the terminal.

* * *

The first fun thing to do in Peru was to go through customs. For some reason the customs inspector decided my camcorder should be declared as professional equipment. It took some discussion for them to determine that I was a tourist and not a journalist or other professional. In the end, I did not have to pay any duty.

It was a little after 2300 when our guide from Tara Tours met us outside customs. We got the baggage loaded in a thirty year old Ford and headed for the Lima Sheraton. Our guide's English was adequate but the driver spoke only Spanish. The two were totally absorbed in the World Cup soccer game on the car radio. Discussion of anything was out of the question over the energetic announcer of the game. Anyway, there was not much to see at that hour on the half-hour ride to the hotel.

Our chariot to the hotel was an old 1960 Ford Galaxy gas hog. Appropriately enough, we ran out of gas on the way to the hotel. Another car stopped to ask if there was a problem. After a short discussion, the other driver opened the trunk of his car. He produced the Peruvian version of our famous west-side credit card—a plastic gallon jug and about four feet of rubber hose. After getting a mouthful of gas, our driver succeeded in siphoning about half a gallon of gas from the other car's tank into the jug. This was put in our car. The gas was paid for, and we were off again. But first, a stop at the local gas station was in order. Gas was 20,000 Intes per liter or about $2.00 a gallon twice the at home price.

The road into town from the combination airport/navy air base was a four-lane divided highway with a raised median. Shoulders of the road were dirt and lined with Eucalyptus trees. The Eucalyptus trees had the bottom four feet of the trunk whitewashed for visibility.

Lima—Welcome to Yesterday

The approach from over the Pacific at night
Gave no clue that we were near
A city—Lima—the capitol of Peru.

No jetway here, it's down those stairs
And a hundred yard walk to the terminal.
Then baggage and customs games.

The tour guide met us
In a 1960 Ford Galaxy.
The driver spoke no English
And had the World Cup Soccer
Broadcasting to the world.

It's after midnight and we are out of gas
So flag down another cab
And siphon a gallon of gas.
Echoes of the 1960's.

*   *   *

The street traversed what appeared to be an industrial area with block-long, ten-foot high, concrete block walls. Some of the walls had guard towers. It is possible that this was some of the military or port complex.

These walls and every other wall we saw had lots of decorations, political posters and advertisements and slogans in the form of graffiti. This was already Saturday morning, and the national election would be held on Sunday. The travel agent had not mentioned being in Peru in the middle of a potentially exciting South American election.

There was no breeze. The humid air was thick with exhaust fumes and photochemical smog. Temperature was about 55 degrees F (12 C). (Almanac records report Lima's average weather to be calm and humid with infrequent rains. This warm, muggy and pollutant-laden air creates a warm polluted bubble or inversion under the cool blanket of air drifting down from the Andes. The resultant acid smog was thick, irritating and very corrosive to Lima's old architecture and outdoor statuary.)

*   *   *

We finally arrived at the Sheridan hotel. As the guide was checking us in, the desk clerk asked if we wanted a black or white room. "What does this mean?" I asked. "With or without a view, naturally," was the haughty reply. I replied, a bit testily, that it was after midnight and dark. Besides we had a 5 AM wake up to get out to the airport for the 7 AM plane to Cuzco. All we wanted was a place to sleep.

We were assigned a "white" room on the fifth floor. It was complete with a hot shower and CNN on the TV giving a rundown on the upcoming election. The view, however, was not impressive. The room overlooked one of the main streets, Passeo de la Republica, and the Plaza de Armas, a World Heritage Site. There was no traffic and very few lights in sight at this hour. (If we could have seen the Plaza we would have had a view of the cathedral and the government buildings. On the southern corner of the plaza Pizarro had been assassinated. In the center was a 15th-centuary bronze statue of a trumpeting angel.)

While Carol prepared for bed, I went down to the lobby for supper and to use our complimentary drink tickets. It was almost one o'clock in the morning. All food service was closed for the night except room service, so I went to the bar. There, with an Aeroperu flight crew, I had a Coke and one of the hotel's famous Pisco sours. Thankfully, the flight crew was not the crew for our flight to Cuzco in about five hours.

It was 11 PM by my time and time to crash.

*   *   *

9 June. Lima to Cuzco

Five AM came early. Oh dark thirty and four hours sleep. At $120 per night plus 13 per cent tax and a 20 per cent overhead charge, the cost of sleep was outrageous. There was also an expected 10-20 per cent tip and a flat 10,000 *Inti* (20 cents) charge per bag carried each way. Maybe I'm just a cheapskate.

A continental breakfast, courtesy of the hotel, was served in the hotel snack bar. This consisted of a selection of toast or rolls, strawberry jelly, fresh (very tart) orange juice and coffee, tea or milk. The snack bar menu listed a hamburger for 200,000 *Inti* and 150,000 *Inti* for our breakfast (at the time the exchange rate was 55,000 *Inti* to a dollar). The hotel's idea of local food included baked sea bass with spicy sauce and deep fried steak with bananas.

*   *   *

Our guide arrived at 6 AM accompanied by a couple from Florida. The "limo" was a rattle VW van that had room for us or the bags but not both. The bags went first with the guide and tickets. We had almost an hour to get acquainted with the other couple. By the time we got to the airport, the guide had our bags checked and boarding passes ready.

The road out to the airport didn't look much better in the early dawn than it had six hours before. Not much traffic was on the road and what was consisted mostly of vehicles dating from the 1960's and 70's. Most of them had the "well used" look with lots of dents and rust. Items like turn signals, wipers and lights appeared not to work. The state of repair of the streets and vehicles did not appear to matter much since the street was not lighted. I don't know what they did on unlighted streets. Many cars and trucks proceeded without lights until they met another vehicle. The only vital item appeared to be the horn. Although most of the signaling at night was done with light or hand signals, much of the daytime signaling was done with beep from the horn.

*   *   *

Bread peddlers (literally) on three-wheeled bicycles with baskets filled with fresh good smelling bread were roaming the streets looking for predawn customers. The less wealthy were standing in line at the bakeries to get the price supported bread. The price went up at 7 AM. After 9 AM, the bakeries could charge whatever the traffic would bear. The regular price of half a dozen rye-and-barley flour rolls was 2,000 *Inti* (two cents each.)

The Bread Man

A lone old man
On a three wheel bicycle
Sold cheap bread
From the basket on the bike
At a floating price of a nickel a loaf.

The peons' stood in line
From seven to nine
For price supported bread
At two cents for rye and barley rolls

At nine AM the price went up
To what ever the market would bear
And the man on the bike went home.

*   *   *

When we arrived at the airport, our luggage had been checked and our boarding passes were ready. The status board showed no schedule changes so we went to the boarding lounge. About 120 people were crowded into a small space with only 30 seats and minimal standing room. Happily, almost no one smoked.

About twenty minutes to boarding time, everyone was required to go outside onto the parking ramp to identify personal baggage to be loaded on the plane. Then, everyone returned to the lounge to await the boarding announcement. At the announcement, everyone crowded up to the gate for the walk across the ramp to the plane. The Peruvians were no different from Americans in that respect. Everyone has reserved seating, so what is the hurry?

Boarding Time in Lima

A hundred people waited
For a 727 to Cuzco
We were called outside to identify
Each piece of baggage to go.

Then back inside to wait some more
While bags were hand-carried to the plane
A hundred yards across the tarmac
in sunshine or in rain.

The plane was an old 737 with no overhead storage or adjustable seats. Later in the flight the stewardess served dinner roll size sandwiches of roast beef or tasteless local cheese and reconstituted orange juice. Just prior to landing we were served a small cup of syrupy coffee.

Our plane taxied past the co-located Peruvian Naval Air Station on our way to the active runway. The Navy had C-130's, Caribous, French helicopters and several miscellaneous high-wing aircraft. There was also a Huey with some kind of antenna in front of the rotor that looked like a shark's fin.

Punching through the clouds we found the morning sun backlighting the Andes. We were over the clouds, so the Pacific Ocean was not visible. Snow pack was the reverse of our northern mountains being on the south slopes of the mountains. All of Peru is south of the equator. Lima is 12 degrees south of the equator at sea level and *Cuzco* at 14 degrees south at 11,152 ft. The date was 5 days before the equinox and the middle of the South American winter.

ANDES SUNRISE

Above the clouds the Andes appeared
Back lit by a morning sun
White snow on southern slopes and a blue-black sky
The Peruvian morning has begun

*   *   *

Peru has always been relatively unpopulated. Several large population centers are separated by vast expanses of sparsely populated mountains and jungle. There are the high, dry *cordilleras* or mountains and the hot, humid and generally unhealthy jungles. The Spanish called the mountain inhabitants *caudillos* and considered them superior because of better living conditions, more and better food and relative freedom from insect borne diseases.

The coastal and lowland Indians were called *costenos* or the coastal people. The *costenos* were relatively smaller people, less healthy and less volatile. The Spanish elite tried to have the best of both by working in the coastal cities but living in the mountains a couple hours away. Commuting to work is nothing new.

*   *   *

5 5:34PM

The flight to *Cuzco* took about 30 minutes. The clouds were quickly left behind. Snow-covered Andes Mountains were ahead and below us framed by a dark blue sky.

Suddenly we were over a high valley. *Cuzco*, the *Quecha* term for the navel or center of the *Quecha* world, occupied the valley floor. The pastel colors of photographs of the area are correct. The roofs were brick red being constructed of reddish clay tiles. The houses were tan adobe block. Hillsides were a patchwork of green fields of winter crops and golden fields of rye and barley ready to cut. Fields and pastures were outlined with dark green lines of Eucalyptus trees.

We passed over the length of a runway that ran half the length of the valley. Then, the plane banked sharply and landed.

CUZCO

Two miles above sea level
Sits Cuzco in a valley,
The navel of the world,
Capitol of the Quecha empire

Red tile roofs on tan adobe walls
Set in green pastures and
Golden fields of barley and rye
Surrounded by mountains
3000 feet high

*   *   *

We walked to the terminal and were met by our tour representatives. I watched the unloading of the 727 from inside the terminal. It was all done by hand. Baggage was stacked unbelievably high on a single wagon and then pushed by several old men to the terminal.

The trip to town was in an old VW bus. Egress from the airport was a narrow brick street. This became a divided street, Avenida del Sol, with Eucalyptus trees and trees they locally called "Retama" planted on the median.

*   *   *

Arrival at the Hotel El Dorado included being ambushed by about twenty peddlers selling coca leaf tea, wool goods, carvings, brass, etc.

The hotel was originally built in art deco style but had been remodeled by various earthquake repairs. The four floors were clustered around a central patio. Much of the patio was occupied by a central elevator tower with stained glass windows. A giant bronze condor hung from the skylight in the roof.

Hotel El Dorado, Cuzco

An art deco structure
Where a huge bronze condor
Hangs in a sky lit atrium.
The elevator passes stained glass
Windows on each floor
Decorated by earthquake residuum

*   *   *

Cuzco is over two miles above sea level. With this in mind, our guides recommended a pot of hot coca tea and a couple hours rest to speed the acclimatization process and prevent altitude sickness. It worked for me.

*   *   *

With all the talk about cocaine and the coca leaf, it was interesting to learn that the Spanish were responsible for this vice being available to the public. In the pre-Columbian Inca days, the common man's vice was alcohol in the form of *chicha*, a corn mash beer. Chewing coca leaf was a privilege reserved for the elite. The puritanical code enforced by the Inca on drinking, eating, sex, and dress served the Inca well. But after the Conquest, the Spanish had everything to gain by keeping the Indian population sedated and chewing coca leaf combined with tobacco and distilled spirits worked quite well.

It was also interesting to learn from our Air Force Intellegence people that the level of cocaine picked up from chewing occasional coca leaf or drinking coca tea would not be detectable by current chemical screening tests.

*   *   *

After a rest and lunch, we started on a tour of *Cuzco* with shopping. We entered a compound containing several boutiques selling pottery, wool, fabrics, jewelry, and leather. These shops had very good quality merchandise.

Cuzco had been the political, military and religious center of the kingdom of *Tahuantinsuyu.* The people called themselves *Quecha.* It was here the Inca or king-priest ruled. The *Quecha* or Inca Empire had replaced its predecessors a bare two hundred years before the Spanish found the New World. According to legend about 1200 A.D. *Manco Capac* married his sister, *Mama Occlo,* and disposed of his three brothers founding the Inca dynasty. With a sacred llama and a golden staff provided by his father, the sun god, he entered the *Cuzco Valley* thrusting his golden staff into the soil. Whenever his staff disappeared into the soil his followers were to drive out the indigenous population and build a city. Seven generations later the Inca or Emperor, Pachacuti Inca Yupanqui (1438-71), and his son, Topa Inca Yupanqui (1471-93) had inherited, conquered or pacified about 380,000 square miles. This was 2400 miles of what are now Ecuador, Peru, western Bolivia, and northern Chile.

*   *   *

Next stop on the tour was the monastery of Santo Domingo. It was built on the foundation of the *Qorikancha,* the *Quechua* Temple of the Sun. The Spanish had entered *Cuzco* in November of 1533 unopposed. They stripped all the gold from the *Quecha* shrines. Twenty per cent of this gold was melted down for shipment to Spain, some went to decorate the new monastery and the remainder was split amongst the conquistadores.

The Spanish built the monastery on part of the original foundation. Some of the stone walls were also retained that the Spanish merely plastered over. Frescoes with religious subjects were painted on the plastered walls. To get back at the Spanish the Indian artists who had been forced to paint Catholic religious scenes put Indian features and clothing on many of the religious figures.

During restoration of the monastery after the earthquake of 1950 the original Inca temple plaza and some of the original temple walls were found intact. In many ways the Indians had been better architects and craftsmen than the Spanish. The temple had been erected using polished stones cut and stacked without the use of mortar and keyed to prevent their moving during an earthquake. The walls are slightly inclined. Windows and doors were trapezoidal and double-framed. Some of the original Inca art was found to be in good condition under the plaster.

The stones were trimmed so as not to allow a credit card to be inserted into the joints. It is still a mystery how the stones weighing as much as 20 tons were jockeyed into place. Probably the general population did manual labor during the time they were not tending the crops. This was the system used by the Mayan.

Broken Church

Monastery of Santo Domingo
Or Qorikanchu, the Temple of the Sun?
The 1950 earthquake undid
What Spanish hands had done.

The Quecha architects built
For earthquake shocks
Polished stones were cut and stacked
Trapezoidal double framed windows
Werc set in the set in these rocks.

The earthquake peeled off
The four hundred year old facade
Revealing the plaza and temple
Dedicated to the sun god.

A crèche in the wall
Held sacred dead Inca bones
Illuminated by Inti Raymi,
The summer equinox sun.

*   *   *

The *Sacsayhuaman* Fortress was the next stop. Situated about two miles from downtown *Cuzco* the fortress is about 200 meters (600 ft) higher and overlooks the valley. It was begun during Inca *Pachacuti's* reign and completed by *Topa* and his son, *Huayna Capac* (1493-1525). The construction was said to have required part-time labor of twenty thousand Indians for eighty years. It had an obvious strategic value to the

Quecha considering the fierce jungle tribes to the east and it provided a symbol fit for the Inca. It also served to keep the lower class busy during the slack farming season. Some of these stones weigh as much as three hundred tons. The stones were mined nearby with stone axes and shaped in the quarry then dragged to the site on log rollers and assembled. (They never invented the wheel.) The three walls are about 1800 feet long and angled to allow crossfire. The original observation towers were destroyed by the Spanish. The fortress had underground passages, reservoirs for water and storerooms for food and weapons that would have allowed the defenders to survive long sieges.

Scaffolding for the pageant of *Inti Raymi* was being erected in the center of the fortress commons. This *Quecha* festival celebrates the summer solstice. It was combined with the Catholic festivals and has now become a *Quecha* homecoming occasion.

A grass from Kenya (called "African grass") had been planted on the site in the 1930's to prevent erosion. A number of alpine wild flowers including lupines, dandelion, mouse ears, and verbena grew among the stones. Some of these plants may be imported exotics. Eucalyptus trees introduced from Australia for firewood invading the hills and replacing some of the original forest.

*   *   *

The puma was the totem of *Cuzco*. Looking down on *Cuzco* from the fortress you could see the outline of the old city in the shape of a puma. The fort was the head and the tail curved outward towards the airport. Legs were formed by the main roads out of the city. The city had out grown its historic boundaries but the main roads still mark the principle features.

*   *   *

The last stop was the so called "Inca Baths". This structure was probably part of the water distribution system for *Cuzco*. Water for drinking and irrigation was impounded and distributed through a series of stone lined canals and hollow log aqueducts.

*   *   *

When we got back to the hotel, Carol had a case of altitude sickness—upset stomach, headache. She had refused the coca tea and hit the street shopping immediately on arrival. She wasn't up to supper.

To add to the fun the electric room heater did not work. Even better, the hotel did not have a converter to reduce their 220 volt system to 110 volts so I could recharge the camcorder batteries.

*   *   *

10 June. *Cuzco* to *Machu Picchu*

At 0500, roosters began to crow. We packed the essentials for an overnight trip to *Machu Picchu* and cleared out of the room. The remaining bags were checked with the hotel until the odyssey resumed. Our continental breakfast in the hotel dining room was of orange or papaya juice, toast and strawberry jelly, tea or coffee.

While we waited for the guides Carol cashed some traveler's checks and bought more Intes. There was a small army of peddlers at the hotel entrance that sold almost anything you could want. Carol attacked, was overwhelmed and forced to buy more jewelry.

The guides arrived and took us to the Santa Anna train station. The area in front of the train station was an open market. There were a lot of stands with fruits, clothing, leather goods and household articles. It was Sunday and Sunday is the principle market day when everyone is in town shopping. It was also Election Day. It was bad planning by our agent to miss market day but this appears to be the normal itinerary. Most tours only allow two or three days to see Cuzco where a week is needed. Time. Money. Interest.

*   *   *

Transportation into the mountains was an electric excursion train with lots of windows. It was supposed to leave at 0700 but this was Election Day and everything was behind schedule. This especially built one car train was complete with a restroom and a snack bar.

Two Peruvian soldiers were on board armed with Uzi machine guns. It was not widely publicized that from the headwaters of the *Urubamba River* to it junction with the Amazon was in the "red zone" where the communist *Sendero Luminosa* or Shining Path Maoist guerrillas were in control.

The trip to *Machu Picchu* took four hours. The first leg was a ride up seven switchbacks from *Cuzco* at 3400m (11,152 ft) to the head of the *Anta Valley* at almost 13,000 ft.

This was typical of the few passes crossing the Andes. Most of the passes are similar to this one—a narrow, winding strip of rocky woodland typically along the course of a mountain stream rushing down from the heights. The foot and mule paths of the past have largely been replaced or are shared by railroads and, more recently, vehicular roads. Steep, circuitous foot trails, stamped out by the passage of countless bare feet, eroded by wind and water over millennia are still the communication links for isolated villages to the outside world and the connection between the jungle and the ocean. It's that or high priced helicopters that have trouble with the altitude.

The *Anta Valley* was rolling farm country that gradually became the valley of the *Urubamba River.* The gorge contains high desert vegetative communities. One community is Cerus peruvianas and the red-leafed bromeliad, *Puya*, stuck to the bare granite walls. Some of the walls were near vertical. Many of the hillsides were crossed by ancient foot trails or held the terraces where crops continued to be raised.

A fellow passenger claimed familiarity with the area. He said he was a retired US Navy officer and a member of the New Orleans Orchid Society and talked of the old days and smuggling orchids and other plants back to New Orleans.

Orchid Smuggling

A retired US Naval officer
Bragged about smuggling orchids in his hat
And has them growing in New Orleans.

He feels no remorse.
The challenge and the prize
Were paramount in his eyes.

*   *   *

The *Urubamba River* is the source of the Amazon. At this level it was cold and swift and raced through a rocky canyon with steep granite sides. Several villages subsist along the river with fields and irrigation systems dating back a thousand years. Terraces and old structures were visible high on the canyon walls. We passed one of the few remaining Indian foot bridges that was still in use. A proposed highway to *Machu Picchu* may proceed along much of this same route some day.

The last few miles along the river were through a high, wooded cloud forest valley with tall trees thickly covered with epiphytes. We reached the power station on the river that fed electricity to *Cuzco*; then, a village with a hot spring and, finally, the station at *Machu Picchu*.

The space for the station shouldered its way into the till at the base of a sheer granite cliff. This massif was tilted almost ninety degrees to the horizontal and rose nearly 2000 ft. almost straight up.

Vendors waited on both sides of the track to pounce on the unwary tourist. After running the gauntlet of vendors, we boarded busses for the trip to the only hotel. The road up the mountainside was 8 Km of switchbacks and climbed 1200 ft to intersect the old *Quecha* trail from *Cuzco* to *Machu Picchu*.

*   *   *

We checked in and found our room. It had hot water, flush toilet and a shower. There was no TV or telephone except in the lounge and neither was very reliable.

We went down to sit on the veranda and eat the sack lunch the tour agency had packed for us. The lunch consisted of cheese sandwiches, fried chicken, an orange, a boiled egg and a bottle of Coke with no opener. (By chance, I had bought a brass llama bottle opener from the gang at the hotel.)

We sat on the terrace in the cool, damp air and watched the convection clouds form and disappear. Warm currents of saturated air rose from the valley gradually cooling until the water vapor suddenly condensed and became visible. They rose several hundred more feet until they were blown away or became too heavy to fly and plunged back into the abyss to begin the cycle over.

Cloud Cycles

Thin wisps
Suddenly appear
That float
And grow
And rise
But then
Like gorged birds
Crash
A thousand feet
To the clouds below

*   *   *

American adventurer Hiram Bingham discovered Machu Picchu in 1911. He thought it was the sacred city of Ucabamba where the Inca had escaped and held off the Spaniards for 35 years. He discovered a group of skeletons that he interpreted as females and decided that these were the Virgins of the Sun who waited on the Inca. All this has been reinterpreted and decided that this was a luxury retreat for the Inca and his staff and that the Spanish never found it.

It appears that the builders of the site came from the farming village of Patallata several miles downstream on the Urubamba River. The question of how the stones were transported to the mountain top was solved by the on-site quarry. Estimates calculate that the construction took about 50 years probably started by Pachacuti Inca Yupanqui (1438-71) in the early part of his rein.

The tour of *Machu Picchu* began after lunch. It was conducted by a Quechua Indian in English and Spanish. The thinking about the origin and uses of *Machu Picchu* has changed since Hiram Bingham found the site. They now have several Indian versions of the Spanish invasion that differ in many respects from the Spanish version.

The most recent details of building *Machu Picchu* say that draining the mountain and terracing had been necessary to stabilize the mountain side since there is about 76 inches of rain and the site is bounded by two faults. They begun at the bottom worked their way upwards. A complex drainage system had to be built to provide drainage and water for drinking and farming.

The old, rounded mountains diffused lighting like the false dawn from an overcast sky, the cool, damp afternoon, the thin air, and the wandering clouds all served to make the visit memorable. The site gave the impression that it had been there forever but recent restorations made only a few months before they were indistinguishable from original *Quecha* rockwork. There was no horizon at times with the end of the world just beyond the rock terrace retaining wall. Then, the mist would clear, and the whole mountain top of bright yellow-green grass and grey stone structures appeared in the foreground against the dark green of *Huaina Picchu*. All this sharply contrasted with the bluegreen mountains across the valley.

Machu Picchu supported an interesting introduced vegetative community. Peach trees and strawberries grew along with dandelions, pepperweed, and several native beans.

An abundance of mosses, liverworts, lichens and ferns thrived in this cool, saturated environment. Venus flytrap plants, <u>Dionaea sp</u>., grew in crevices in the rock wall. Gladiolas, naturalized at some time in the past, flashed a vivid red. Several species of native Begonia were in pale pink bloom.

About sundown, I took a walk down and around a couple switchbacks. Another <u>Solanum</u>, <u>S</u>. <u>muricatum</u>, also called *Pepino*, was common along the road. It grew to be 8-10 ft tall with pale blue-white flowers. The potato, <u>Solanum</u> <u>tuberosum</u>, originated in these mountains.

There were a couple small yellow mallows and small yellow composites. A tall flower that resembled <u>Pentstemmon</u> and a pretty speckled <u>Calceolarius</u> were growing along a stream. <u>Fuchsia magellanica</u> was growing at the base of the road cut along with several orchids. A bush had flowers that looked like <u>Lapageria sp</u>. or a large cigarette flower. I heard an occasional toad or tree frog call and several birds were settling in for the night. By the time I got back it was dark. Bats and goatsuckers were diving around the only street light.

*   *   *

*   *   *

As we waited for the dining room to open a couple other guests and I discussed local politics and such with the three soldiers. This had been Election Day and the guards were ready for anything with their machine guns. The communist *Sendero Luminosa* or Shining Path Maoist guerrillas were active and their favorite targets were small remote power plants, large electric transmission towers and isolated tourist.

I asked one of the guards to point out the Southern Cross but the clouds were in the way.

Carol still wasn't feeling well so I had supper and turned in.

It began to rain and rained softly all night.

*   *   *

11 June. Machu Picchu to Cuzco

It was still raining at 0600 and 0700. By 0800, the rain had stopped. Carol still wasn't feeling too well, but we took a walk down the road to the first switchback. It was light but completely overcast with visibility at a half mile. White morning glories were open covering an old building. Growing in mud and standing water in and along a narrow drainage channel beside the road were <u>Hydrocotyle</u>, three species of Oxalis (probably *O*. <u>carnosa</u>, <u>O</u>. <u>hedysaroides</u> and <u>O</u>. <u>herrerae</u>), a clover, sow thistle (?) and an Acanthaceae that looked like shrimp plant (<u>Belopherone sp</u>.). We went back to the hotel and checked out, and Carol spent most of the day sleeping.

The clouds came and went, but *Machu Picchu* was not visible. I had wanted to get up early and photograph the sun coming up over the site, but the sun never came up.

*   *   *

About noon, a group of barefoot Indians came down out of *Machu Picchu*. They had huge packs. Bundles or wooden crates were slung across their backs contained in colorful wool blankets. I asked the guard who they were and where they were going. He told me that they were

"*Mercantadores*" or porters. They carried almost everything needed to and from the mountain villages on their backs. There were no roads in the mountains only the old trails. The trail down to the railway was 2 KM straight down the hill and the descent took these hardy people about 20 minutes. Then they gathered at a camp ground near the river for a rest and a meal before beginning a three day trek by trail to *Ollantaitambo*.

Mercantadores

A dozen men in knee high pants
And sleeves rolled up above the elbow
Came out of the mist
With crates strapped to their shoulders
Or huge packs slung in a colorful red cloth
Knotted over their forehead.
Barefooted or with leather sandals
They walk the Inca trails
Between the small farming villages
Providing everything needed
From the outside world
And the latest gossip, too.
Ten miles a day two miles high
Coca leaf makes the time fly.

*   *   *

I asked Carol if she could handle the bags and come down on the bus. She said she could, so I packed two cameras, binoculars and notebook and started down the trail after the Indians.

In a couple minutes, the Indians were out of sight. I took my time looking and shooting pictures. The trail was a series of short, narrow switchbacks. Some of the trail was pounded several feet into the hillside by bare Indian feet. There were also a number of stone stepped descents. The stones were inserted into the hillside to form a stairway. The trails were maintained by families as part of their taxes. The trail, as a whole, provided very stable footing.

Imagine the work of building and maintaining this trail! Clearing the right-of-way must have been arduous. Keeping the jungle growth from reclaiming the trail was and will continue to be labor intensive. Laying stones for steps that weighed up to a couple hundred pounds each required a great deal of labor. These stones were carried up from the river by hand and set in place. Switchbacks had originally been dug by hand using sticks and stone tools. Slaves probably did all the work and then were forced to use the trail to carry everything needed for commerce.

In some places, ferns similar to Bracken (Pteridium sp.) draped over the trail. There was a cool, damp, organic smell like fresh potting soil. Other sections of the trail were open to the sky with fantastic views of the jungle covered, faulted granite monolith across the river standing on its edge, of clouds rising and falling on the temperature changes and of the river valley below. Several isolated parcels of ancient terraced fields predated the structures on the top. Crops once raised remained visible as if they might still be used as well they may.

Bare granite inclines beside the trail were covered with the red bromeliads, Puya alpestris, recently past their peak bloom. A few Puya were still in bloom with stalks of dark blue flowers.

At least three different orchids were in bloom. What looked like wild ginger was also just past blooming. Coffee berries were bright red on their trees. Begonias (B. coccinea?) were in bloom everywhere. Tall grass dominated and stabilized the steep hill sides.

Vegetative communities gradually changed from tropical alpine to the tropical cloud forest. Wish I had more references and time.

Farther down the trail the tropical trees and vines became more common. There were masses of ferns that looked like Boston fern. On the wet rock walls were polypodium ferns, mosses, liverworts and selaginella.

Along the trail near the bottom was a delicate evening primrose with perfect half-inch wide pink flowers. A vine with four inch long heart-shaped leaves sprouted two-inch purple flowers. A single Indian Paint Brush (Castilleja sp.) grew in the course grass at the end of the trail.

Along the river, strawberry plants grew with tiny yellow fruit. Oxalis, Hydrocottyle, ferns and a different specie of Begonia with large, crenate leaves sprouted from the base of the river's high water berm. Tall, bare trees covered with epiphytes grew in open shade along the water's edge. Hibiscus and small bushes of several small mallows grew in cultivation along with kapok, bread fruit, pumello, papaya and coffee.

It took me almost an hour to loaf down the trail looking and shooting pictures. Other than the Indians that had disappeared, the only humans I saw were two little boys who ran up and down the trail racing the busses coming down the switchbacks. They hollered at the busses as the busses crossed the trail and the tourists hollered back.

*   *   *

It was time for lunch so I bought two bananas, a pumello and an Incacola for about fifty cents. Inca Cola is not bad. It's the Peruvian equivalent of a Mexican soda called Bimbo or our own Mountain Dew.

It was a couple hours before the bus was due so I visited with the vendors and talked with the kids. Two little boys pointed out plants and birds and played songs on their flutes. I watched birds [small sparrow-like birds, some small, all white Least Terns (Sterna albifrons), and a Mountain Wren (Troglodytes solstitalis)], listened to the sound *Urubamba River* with its rushing white water and walked along the river's edge to pick up some stones for the collection.

The sun had disappeared behind the mountains when bus got in about 5 PM. The train left at 5:30 in the dark. We passed the overnight camp of the *mercantadores.*

There was little to see on the way back to *Cuzco* in the swinging headlight of the train but a slow, cold mist. We arrived in Cuzco about 8:30.

*   *   *

Back at the hotel in Cuzco, the TV in the lobby announced that Fujimori had won the election. The *Sendero Luminosa* guerrillas set off a bomb near the Cuzco military barracks in protest.

We had supper and went to bed early so we could be up at 5 AM to begin the next leg of the trip.

Our room was on the top floor this time. It had a vaulted ceiling and stained glass windows. A tile dido had once run around the room but most of it had been shaken loose by earthquakes. There was a crèche with nothing in it and a funny little door that opened into a closet half the size of the room.

*   *   *

12 June. Cuzco to Iquitos

A local rooster and the alarm both went off about 0500. We finished packing and checked out right after breakfast. I was getting the bags down to the lobby when I heard someone fire off a clip of bullets from an AK-47 automatic rifle. I mentioned it to our fellow guests but no one else admitted hearing anything. The staff indicated that such things happened occasionally.

Breakfast was good or maybe I was hungry. During breakfast, we noticed that much of the hand carved wooden trim in the dining room had been painted over—such a crime.

*   *   *

Transportation arrived at 0800 for our 9 o'clock flight. On the way to the airport, we noticed that trucks were stopping to pick up passengers. Our driver explained that the bus drivers were on a protest strike.

Our route took us by the military barracks where the bomb had gone off. There was no obvious damage, and no one had been injured.

*   *   *

Our airline, Aeroperu, was right on schedule—an hour late.

The flight was smooth, and the mountains were beautiful. Long shafts of sunlight pierced the clouds at times. Snow was heavy on the southern slopes with large snow fields hanging precariously over several deep, narrow valleys. The valleys were generally oriented east-west with a silver thread of a river snaking along the valley floor. As we went farther northwest towards Lima less snow was visible on the Pacific slopes.

We crossed several deep valleys—the Apurimac R. that feeds the Amazon; the Ica with the cities of *La Oroya* and *Ica*; the Pisco River in the *Acucacu Valley* to *Pisco*; the *Canete* and *Huancayo Rivers*; and the *Paracas Peninsula* under the clouds. Then out over the Pacific Ocean for the approach to Lima.

The abrupt changes in topography and altitude are a unique feature of the Andes. The wealthy could work in the heat and humidity of a tropical jungle farming community on the valley floor near sea level but be in the cool, dry, barren mountains in a couple hours.

Out over the Pacific the plane turned to begin its approach into Lima. We were in the clouds and never saw the water.

* * *

The plane arrived an hour late but, to make up for it, the plane for Iquitos was rescheduled from 1100 to 1300 then to 1500. Since we had several hours, our guide took us into Lima to see at least some of the sights.

One of the last pre-Inca cultures developed near Lima. *Chancay*, located on the coast 35 miles north of Lima, was the artistic center of a subculture of the *Chimu Empire*. The kingdom was known as the *Cuismancu*. Its principal city was *Cajamarquilla* just up the *Rimac River* from Lima. *Chancay* was famous for the moon goddess statues, textiles with bold geometric designs and for black-on-white pottery with "optical" checkerboard designs of dots and lines. This culture existed from about 1000 to 1400 AD.

Lima was Pizarro's capitol of the new world. After sacking *Cuzco*, Pizarro decided that the *Quecha* capitol was not suitable for his administrative center. He needed communication with Spain, so he established Lima which translates as "City of Kings." Lima was ten miles from the anchorage, later the seaport, of *Callo* on the delta of the *Rimec River*. This is one of the few river valleys on the Pacific side of the Andes capable of supporting a large population.

The *Plaza de Armas* was the site where Pizarro was supposed to have drawn the map of the new city on the ground with his sword. That was in 1535. This was the second time Pizarro drew a magic line. Eight years before, in 1527, he had drawn a line for those who would accompany him to Peru. Thirteen accepted, and the rest returned to Panama. Pizarro and his group found *Tumbes* on the Incas northern frontier. They saw advanced architecture and a well-organized government. Fine wool textiles and worked gold and silver were more than enough to convince him that more would be available farther south.

Pizarro returned to Spain in 1528 and got the backing of King Charles V. He returned to Panama in 1528 as Governor and Captain-General of Peru and *adelantado* or agent of the Church and King. He was accompanied by his four brothers and some volunteers from his home town of Extremadura, Spain. In late 1530, he left Panama with 180 men and 27 horses for Ecuador. They marched south long the coast until November of 1532 when they arrived at the *Quecha* capitol of *Cajamarca*.

Atahualpa, the Inca, had recently won a civil war defeating his cousin and imprisoning him in *Cuzco*. Pizarro requested an audience during which a priest lectured *Atahualpa* on the supremacy of the Pope and the King of Spain. At a signal, the Spanish fired on the crowd and took the Inca prisoner. For two months, the *Quecha* Indians brought gold to fill a room as a ransom for *Atahualpa*. Pizarro then accused Atahualpa of treason, condemned him to death and baptized him. The Inca was executed by strangulation, and Pizarro headed for *Cuzco*.

*   *   *

The government palace and the main post office of Lima front on the plaza as does the present cathedral. The city was virtually destroyed by the earthquakes of 1687 and 1746. A new cathedral was built each time on the original foundation.

We toured the cathedral and saw Pizzaro's tomb. In 1537, Pizarro had defeated Almargo, one of his oldest friends, and had him strangled. In 1541, Pizarro was assassinated by a band of Almargo's men. Francisco Pizarro, an illegitimate child of peasant background, ruler of all South America, died at an old age of near 70 years.

Pizarro was a late bloomer and a victim of serendipity. Columbus and later explorers had killed or enslaved most of the Indians on the Caribbean islands. Cortes wiped out the Aztecs and northern Mexican culture. Alvarado killed a million Mayans and subjugated Central America. But there were still rumors of gold, and Pizarro wanted his.

The Conquistador's Excuse

The Conquistadors consuming greed
was disguised
and excused by the need
to convert or kill the infidel
who would not accept the Catholic creed.
European diseases
gave genocide God's speed.

*   *   *

The forty year old Pizarro was an illiterate farmer from Trujillo, Spain near Estremadura. He joined the gold rush in 1510 and met Cortes, a distant relative, in Hispaniola but decided to join Balboa. He was with Balboa in 1511 when the Pacific was discovered. He was shown some gold trinkets and a drawing of a llama.

In 1523, Pizarro was in Darien (Panama) under the supervision of the incompetent Pedrarias Davila, Balboas' successor. Pizarro owned a parcel of swamp and a *repartimento* of belligerent Indians. Frustrated, he joined forces with an old friend, Diego de Almagro and a priest, Hernando de Luque, in outfitting the first of three explorative voyages along the coast of Ecuador.

The first and second voyages were near disasters. The third voyage landed on the Island of Gallo in 1527 where his famous line in the sand separated men from boys and launched the conquest of the Incas.

The Cathedral contained massive and intricate carvings in its many chapels. The work must have occupied many Indian sculptors for a lifetime. The museum in the Archbishops' palace holds carvings and paintings by Indian artists. The Indians portrayed Mary and Christ with Indian features.

*   *   *

Next stop on this whirlwind tour was the National Museum of Anthropology and Archeology. There had been a guerrilla attack on the electrical transmission lines into Lima in response to the election results. Electrical service to the museum was cut, and the lights were off when we started the tour. We got a personal private tour by flashlight. The lights came on half way through the tour.

The museum was very well organized with displays in chronological order. *Chavin de Huantar* from 850-300 B.C. with its cat god cult was the earliest culture. Crude pottery replaced gourds. Corn and potatoes became dietary staples. Cotton cloth replaced pounded bark clothing. The llama and alpaca were domesticated. The relative peace between 300 B.C. and 200 A.D. allowed the arts to flourish around *Nazca* and the *Paracas Peninsula*. The *Nazca* lines were probably astronomical observatories. Next major culture was the *Moche* about 400 A.D. and lingering until about 1000 A.D. when the *Tiahuanaco* invaded from Bolivia and the *Lake Titicaca* area. The *Moche* was naturalist artists of portrait pottery. Architecture and medicine flourished. The explicit sexual art of the Moche was also memorable. The Tiahuanaco were noted for the crying figures. The Kingdom of *Chimor* absorbed the *Mochicas* that were left. The elegant polished blackware and gold smithing were the major legacy of the Chimor. Then came the Incas. The displays were very good. Wish there had been more time but an hour is better than nothing.

*   *   *

Back at the airport, we found the flight delayed further. We had been scheduled to be in Iquitos for lunch and a tour of Iquitos. We had lunch in the airport and the plane finally left at 8 PM.

A snack bar in the airport had hamburgers on the menu. The burgers came open faced and tasted like a strong meatloaf. Local yellow potatoes were used for the fries. These tasted sweet—more like fried yams. About sundown, we tried the Peruvian version of an ice cream parlor for a coke and a dish of ice cream. Their idea of a dish of ice cream was three big scoops—almost a pint. I had mango and Carol had vanilla. That quality of the ice cream would never sell in San Antonio.

Carol ran out of reading material. And, since we had been to all the boutiques several times, she bought a Miami Herald for two dollars. We devoured this newspaper until the plane finally left.

We watched a Russian Aeroflot Illusion airliner from Havana landed and unloaded about a hundred passengers.

Boarding the plane was like boarding the one to Cuzco except it was in the dark of night. The plane had only one overhead storage compartment so most of the packages and carry-on luggage was stacked in and under seats. The door of the overhead bin swung in the breeze the whole trip. Luckily, nothing fell out.

There was a stop in *Pucallpa*. The 727 landed with the flight deck door open. I could see the runway lights from our seats in the rear of the plane. Another half hour flight over absolute blackness and we landed in Iquitos.

*   *   *

Iquitos, an island of light in the velvet black, was completely isolated from the rest of the world for access by land. The only ways in or out of town for everything was by the Amazon or by air. It was surprising to see so many cars and trucks.

The tour representatives picked us and another couple up at the baggage counter. Downtown was about three miles to the southeast of the airport along the river. Traffic was light but then it was 11 PM. Most of the traffic was motorcycles and motorcycle taxis. They drove all over the road which was a narrow two lane blacktop roadway.

The Hotel Turista was an aging four story hotel overlooking the Amazon and Padre Isla. We unpacked, and I plugged in the battery charger for the camcorder batteries (I discovered the charger would work on anything from 90 to 240 volts AC or DC). Carol was tired, and I was hungry. She went to bed, and I went out to eat.

An open air restaurant a block down the street was alive with light and Indian music. Several tables of American and Canadian students appeared to have had a beer too many. A five-piece Indian band was playing local songs with flute and drums. I ordered a dish called *Gallo Saltada*. Very good. After a while, the musicians left and so did I.

*   *   *

So far on this trip we missed scheduled tours of Lima and Iquitos. We also missed the Sunday market day in *Cuzco*. A no cost extra was being scheduled in *Cuzco* on election weekend with most businesses closed and the Army very visible with their automatic weapons. Looking ahead, we would be in Buenos Aires over a national holiday when most things would be closed. Then there was Pizzaro's children's airline! Aeroperu had a practiced inability to keep schedules. For this trip travel agents and tour companies' rank close to car salesmen and politicians in credibility.

* * *

13 June. Iquitos and the Amazon Camp

I woke up at 0600 with the breaking dawn. It was still a few minutes before sunrise. As I looked out the window, several Greater Ani (<u>Crotophaga</u> <u>major</u>) were picking up crickets and other insects on the ledge outside our window. A Gray-capped Flycatcher (<u>Myiozetetes</u> <u>grandensis</u>) was filling up on blackflies and other insects from a perch high in a mango tree across the street. I turned the air conditioner off and opened the window to hear the Amazon sunrise. The flycatcher was announcing his territorial boundaries, and the tree frogs were finishing their night of calls of impending love. It was not quite the cacophony I had expected from an Amazon sunrise.

AMAZON SUNRISE

Sunrise on the Amazon
Did not assault the senses
But slipped in on the dying night sounds
As the light increased in slow increments.

Parrot-like Greater Ani
Chased crickets
On the ledges outside the windows.

Trilling of frogs
And polymorphic insect noises
Disappeared in the humidity
As day began.

A White-capped Flycatcher
Perched on a erect mango branch
Sprang upward through a cloud of blackflies
Staking his claim and calling for a mate.

*   *   *

About 7 AM, vendors began appearing along the street across from the hotel getting a head start on the day. One was a woman with a tray of *empenadas*. Another was a man with a wheeled stand that sold gum, razor blades and other small items you might want.

*   *   *

We went down for breakfast (fried eggs with Nescafe hot chocolate) and then out to see this world. We crossed the street to look at the Amazon and then walked around the block. It was only 8 AM and nothing was open. The Plaza de Armas was empty of people but full of tropical pastel color. A large African Tulip tree (<u>Spathodea</u> <u>campanulata</u>) was in full bloom. Manila and other palms studded the plaza. Red Hibiscus (<u>Hibiscus</u> <u>rosa-sinensis</u>) was colorful and conspicuous flashes of color. A fountain in the center of the plaza was three tiered and painted pink and lime green. The third tier featured a large pink dolphin atop a shaft that looked as if he was skewered through his belly button. The cathedral and the Rio Amazonas office both fronted on the plaza.

Along the river Bananas (<u>Musa</u> <u>spp</u>) and big green-leafed Taro (<u>Colocasia</u> <u>esculenta</u>) were cultivated. Multifarious shades of green were the majority.

We stopped a taxi and took a ride to the end of civilization—the port of *Belem*. The taxi was ancient and well used with a windshield so dirty that it was difficult to take pictures through it. This was the port area, a stilt village called, "the Venice of the Amazon." The street into the area was one way. Much of the street was one lane and full of ruts and holes. It was shared by motorcycles, trucks, bicycles and pedestrians. We stopped several times for trucks to edge past or for people, loaded with chickens or a stalk of bananas, to cross the street.

The Belem Market

People everywhere in the cool of dawn,
Produce to market and products back home
Carried on the backs or heads of Indians and Creoles
Before it gets hot and the sun, humidity and flies rise.
Displayed on palm leaf mats, everything you need-
Fish, chickens, rice, bananas, voodoo charms
And they can fix your motorbike too.

* * *

People were everywhere in the relative cool of dawn. The sun and flies would drive them back home soon. Most of the produce was carried on backs or balanced on the heads of pedestrians. Bags of rice and stalks of green bananas were on backs or shoulders. Unidentifiable bundles, crates and other containers were balanced or supported on the head.

In Mecardo Belem, the market place, were endless stalls and small shops. Most of the material for sale was displayed on banana leaves or palm leaves spread on the edge of the street. Shops or street vendors sold anything sellable—bananas, cheap plastic goods, live or fresh killed chickens and hogs, fresh fish, dried fish, native herbal medicine. They could even repair your motorcycle and outboard motor while you waited.

The vendors and shops stopped at what was probably the high water mark. The buildings were on pilings that got taller as we descended into the flood plain of the Amazon. High water marks on the poles showed that the water line was 10-12 feet above the ground. Finally, there was no more road so the driver turned around and returned along the same route.

Apparently, everyone had to carry his/her own weight. An old man was crossing the street with an enormous stalk of bananas. He stumbled and dropped his load. Traffic stopped and several people helped him get the load back on his back, but no one offered any other assistance.

*   *   *

By the time we got back to the Plaza de Armas, it was 9 o'clock, and the stores were open. I bought another video tape and two more rolls of film. Half a block from the hotel, we found a shop that sold local handicrafts. Items included local jewelry, stuffed piranhas, and pictures on tapa cloth (Mulberry bark), postcards, and pottery. There were also some of the Inca pottery and wool items from the mountains. We picked out our treasures and returned to the hotel to checkout and meet our guide.

Across the street from the hotel was the Maloka restaurant that looked out over the Amazon. It wasn't open but we walked over to look at their view. Bananas, taro and miscellaneous vines and shrubs rushed down the steep river bank down to the mud flats. The river was about twenty feet low since June is the middle of the Amazon winter dry season. Rice had been broadcast over the mud flats which wcre turning lush green.

BELEM

Called the Venice of the Amazon
Belem is built mud, and stilts and
of floating homes that ground
on the mudflats of the Amazon summer.

Roofs thatched and patched with tin,
electric lines strung on trees and
on poles shared with vultures.

A raft of logs serves as a lawn
where children play,
and planks are sidewalks
floating on a sea of mud.

*   *   *

Thatch roofed houseboats had been grounded in various locations. Their 24 VDC or 240 VAC electricity was delivered by wires tied or nailed to poles pushed into the mud. Most of these power poles had a vulture perched on the poles' top. Two large flocks of vultures were gathered on the mud for separate feasts.

Log platforms formed the front yard of some of the houses. Catwalks made of logs on top of the mud lead to water deep enough to float a boat. Some of the thatched roofs were patched with tin sheets. Several structures that looked like privies were located on some of the catwalks some distance from the houses.

*   *   *

Transportation arrived at 10 AM. It was the same old Ford that had transported us to the hotel on the previous night. The tour people would pick up the bags later and deliver them to the M/V Rio Amazonas.

The Ford drove down the morning's route, then farther to a dock on the Nanay River. The road was a single lane, rutted trail that ran right to the water's edge. Temporary tin covered sheds lined the road. Users of the landing had the opportunity to purchase snow cones, fruit, vegetables, fish, etc. fresh or cooked by local vendors. The water had receded another five feet since the sheds had been installed. Flotsam identified the water line—plastic, citrus peels and other trash. Modern floodlight standards along the road were a contrast to the otherwise primitive third-world setting.

Children and dogs played in the potholes full of water and along the edge of the river. Several children were paddling small canoes in the shallow water.

We crossed down the muddy incline and boarded the ferry to the Amazon Camp. Up the gang plank and duck under the thatched roof of the boat. The boat was about 6 feet wide and 25 feet long with a square stern and a 25 hp OMC motor.

*   *   *

The boat backed out, and we started up the Nanay River. We passed a local oil refinery and a ship yard, past the country club and its golf course and another half hour up the brown Nanay River to the Amazon Camp. We overtook several small canoes with fishermen pulling gill nets along the rivers' edge. A number of other canoes using the river contained family groups and produce on the way to or from market.

Amazon Camp came into sight as a pair of thatched roofs in the trees. Constructed of large floating logs with some planks lashed to their tops, the boat landing floated on the water rising and falling with the flow of the river. We off-loaded and climbed twenty feet up a wooden stair to a large, thatch-covered room with only a guard rail for walls. Here we met our guide, a spider monkey and a marmoset. A green parrot and a Scarlet Macaw (<u>Ara</u> <u>macao</u>) were also present but not very sociable. The monkeys were immediately into everything anyone left unattended.

Lunch consisted of fried fish, taro, palm salad, slices of banana and mango. Iced tea or Inca Cola was available to drink. After lunch, the guide briefed us on our upcoming short trek through the jungle.

On the edge of the river bank and out over the river were three-foot long purse-shaped nests of Green Oropendola (<u>Psarocolius</u> <u>viridis</u>) hanging from the branches of a tall Cecropia tree (<u>Cecropia</u> <u>sp</u>). Parrots were screaming in the distance across the river.

A canoe with four armed soldiers motored past up river. A few minutes later, a long canoe came down stream containing five adults and several children. It also contained several plastic coolers filled with fish and many bunches of green bananas.

*   *   *

As we gathered in a clearing behind the dining room, the guide pointed out various trees—banana, Cecropia, red kapok (<u>Ceiba pentandra</u>), etc. A vulture with wings spread was sunning itself in the top of a large red kapok tree.

The spider monkey decided to come along for the walk. He wanted to be carried. Since no one would carry him, he climbed vines and jumped on everyone. The path or trail lead first, through second growth jungle. A slash and burn field was slowly becoming jungle again. The jungle was absorbing relic banana plants, ginger and other field and door-yard plants crops. The path was well worn and lead to a village about a quarter mile from the camp.

The village consisted of four thatched structures. Each house consisted of a covered platform raised on poles about five feet off the ground. A notched log served as a stair. The house consisted of an enclosed room about eight by twelve feet wide and a roofed open space about ten by twelve feet. The walls were made of light weight poles of a local mallow plant. The roof was made of overlapping layers of nippa palm fibers. There were about seven courses of the fibers capped with a ridge cap of woven palm leaves. The open area was protected by railings of wood lashed to the uprights. A separate small cook shack behind the main structure provided a place to safely store and prepares food without danger of burning the house down.

Dogs, hogs, and chickens rested under the houses out of the sun. Clothing hung on the railings and on lines strung across the porch. Children played in a hammock slung on the porch. Additional hammocks hung triced up waiting for nightfall.

We continued through the village to an open field. Indians in native dress met us with native jewelry, blowguns and other items for trade. One of the men demonstrated how to handle a blowgun and let us try. He hit the banana tree target two out of three shots. I hit the base of the target on the second try.

The monkey tried to get at the trade goods strung on a line, and the children did their best to keep him away. They harassed the monkey, and the monkey responded by climbing our legs rather than up the nearby trees.

A quick walk and we were back at the camp. We passed through another field being taken back by the jungle. Some small trees were appearing along the edge of the field but swordgrass was taking over most of the open areas. Swordgrass would probably remain the dominant vegetation for some time.

* * *

Back at the camp, everyone rehydrated and enjoyed a coke or beer. We relaxed, bought souvenirs and got acquainted while waiting for the transportation back to Iquitos to board the M/V Rio Amazonas.

An addition to our group was a school teacher from Ft. Worth. She had been staying at the camp. She had made several trips to the area and was photographing and collecting artifacts for a book on primitive art.

The trip back down the Nanay was uneventful. We off-loaded into several vintage automobiles and went to the main dock area. The M/V Rio Amazonas and several local ferry boats snuggled together. They were connected to the shore and each other by a series of planks.

* * *

We boarded the ship and were shown to our room. Our luggage was in the room on the bunks. The suite consisted of three spaces. There was an 8 X 10 foot room with two bunks, shelves for life preservers and two 28 volt lamps. The bath was 4 X 6.5 feet and serviced by river water. A two liter bottle of potable water was provided for drinking. The bathroom had a 220 VAC receptacle. The entrance hall was 3.5 X 4 feet and contained two air conditioning ducts in the ceiling. We had a porthole covered with a cloth shade.

A get acquainted meeting was held in the lounge. We were introduced to the captain and crew and to our guide, Beder Chavez. Other passengers included an Army Reserve Colonel Story and his wife from New Orleans, a couple from New York, an engineer from New

Jersey, the school teacher from Ft Worth, a retired Amazon riverboat captain and his wife and a German national and his Peruvian girl friend.

We left the dock just before sunset and watched the sun disappear into red and orange clouds over the skyline of Iquitos and the Eiffel Hotel. Dinner was at 8 PM.

*   *   *

14 June. Down the Amazon

I was up at 0500, before the sun. I took a camera up to the bow to photograph the Amazon sunrise. The *Rio Amazonas* was moored to a tree near the mouth of the *Rio Apayacu*. I was a little surprised there were no mosquitoes or black flies. The temperature was about 72 degrees F. I did some yoga stretching and went through the first three Shotokan katas twice.

It was just getting light and the world was still and pastel. The sun was fighting its way through a cloud bank. It finally lit up the tree tops then rapidly painted the world with sunshine down to the very river.

Amazon Morning

From the bow the Amazon River
Was flat as a mirror.
Not a breath stirs in the false dawn.

The sun fights its way
Through a cloud bank and
The first bright rays
Lit up the tree tops.

Along the rivers edge
A lone fisherman tended his nets
From a dugout canoe.
A vee-shaped wake
Points to a canoe with a man and woman.
The dipping paddles just audible
Across the water.

*   *   *

In the distance drifted a canoe with a fisherman working the edge of an island in the river. Another canoe paddled by a man and woman crossed the river 200 yards off our bow, leaving a sharp Vee of ripples to mark its passage.

*   *   *

By the time the sun came out, everyone was up and ready for an 0600 birding trip up the *Rio Apayacu*. We loaded into two aluminum boats for the trip. The water was so still and flat it was difficult to tell the water from the sky.

We were out for about an hour and saw a number of birds. The Oropendola or weaver bird always builds its nest hanging over the water. Wattled Jacanas (Jacana jacana) were walking on vegetation at the water's edge. There were also Yellow-backed Oriole (Icterus chrysater), a Black-Collared Hawk (Busarellus nigricollis) and a Gray Hawk (Buteo nitidus). Several Ring-billed Kingfishers (Ceryle torquata) flew across the river while Gray-capped Flycatcher (Myiozetetes grandensis) and Black-tailed Flycatcher (Myiobus articaudus) made looping forays against blackflies. A Hermit Hummingbird family (Phaethornis sp.) worked its way along the river bank looking for flowers. Several pairs of Yellow-Headed Parrots (Amazona ochrocephala) and Toucanettes (Aulacorhynchus sulcatus) flew over; the parrots were always seen flying in pairs. An Oven Bird (Seiurus aurocapillus) was building a nest on a small branch out over the water. We heard several Horned Screamers (Anhima cornuta). Their calls reverberated through the trees and carried a long way on the still air.

A single sloth was spotted on this trip. It was high in the small limbs of a Cecropia tree and visible only as a dark silhouette against the light gray sky. It moved slowly. It took a short time to tell that it had moved.

Many trees grew along the river. Most of them had the ability to grow partially submerged for part of the year. The trees are covered with vines and epiphytes. Bromeliads, aroids, orchids, and Philidendron abound. Members of the Melastomaceae, Piperaceae, Discorea, Marantaceae, Passiflora, and Gesneriaceae were common.

* * *

We caught up with the Rio Amazonas and had breakfast while steaming up the Apayacu River to our next stop. This was the village of Pucaurquillo shared by the Bora and Huitoto Indians. These two tribes were closely related like cousins and have similar but distinct customs and languages. They both migrated from the state of Amazonas in Columbia in the 1930's where the Indians had been virtual slaves to the rubber barons. They were paid little to collect wild rubber from the jungle, but were harshly punished for not meeting stiff quotas. Penalties included disfigurement and mutilation. The Peruvians were probably not much better as humanitarians than the Colombians but whole tribes did not migrate to Colombia.

Our guide escorted us into the village through a field of grass and chiggers. We passed thatched huts on either side of a graded dirt road. Sisal fiber hung on poles drying in the sun. Most of the houses were as described for the village near the Amazon Camp. One of the houses was unusual in that it had a second story. Also, several sheets of corrugated metal roofing formed part of its siding.

A few children walked down the street with us. We stopped by several of the houses where children swung in hammocks as their mothers looked on. All the children appreciated chocolate and one member of our party obliged them with M&M's.

Our guide led us to a large, circular pole framed building with a thatched roof. Most of the villagers were waiting for us with trade goods on display. The structure covered about 4000 square feet. The walls were of straight saplings spaced and tied about an inch apart. The eight foot wide gate was similarly constructed. The gable ends were open and oriented to catch any transient breezes.

Trade goods included carved gourds (Kataka or penis guards) and handmade jewelry made of feathers, seeds, clam shells, piranha jaws, etc., strung on sisal fibers. There were also pictures of birds and animals drawn with natural dyes on the inner bark of a ficus tree and carved parrots. Some of the pictures we saw later contained unnatural colors that came from a felt-tip pen. Baskets and items such as canoe paddles and blow guns were also for sale or trade. They mostly wanted to trade for dollars. We bought a several items and I traded baseball caps for a few other items.

One of the most common necklace materials was the tall skinny acai (Euterpe oleracea) a palm raised for food and herbal properties. Another was the Pau-Brazil (Caesalpinia echinata) a timber tree.

A couple of girls about ten had dressed up and put on some lipstick they had traded for. I let them to look at the playback through the camcorder. They were tickled to see themselves on tape.

Most of the Bora adults wore native attire. Men wore a loin cloth and headband. The women wore only a knee-length skirt. The material was the inner bark of the ficus tree. Decorations on the ficus bark cloth was brown vegetable dye and looked like a geometric coiled snake.

These Indians appeared to be in good physical condition. They were brown-skinned, small—5'4" or less—and thin with straight black hair. They had few scars from accidents or disease but no tattoos or ceremonial scars. All had the mongoloid mark, a bluish area over the kidneys. Many of the adults had broken or missing teeth.

*   *   *

The MEDCAP had reported an outbreak of dengue began in the *Punchaua* port area near Iquitos in April. Between 100,000 and 150,000 cases were reported to the World Health Organization along with several hundred cases of hemorrhagic dengue fever from southwest Venezuela. Besides dengue, the DVDP noted three types of malaria, yellow fever and several internal parasitic infections including leishmenisis are endemic to the upper Amazon. None of these were obvious in these people.

We had our shots updated before we left—yellow fever, tetanus, typhoid, cholera, polio and plague—and had a gamaglobulin shot for good measure. A course of weekly chloroquine tablets for malaria was started two weeks before we left San Antonio and would continue this for a month after we left the Amazon. Fansidar tablets were also available in our emergency supplies in case of onset of malaria symptoms. These emergency supplies also included Pepto tablets, DEET insect repellent, Neosporin ointment, Bactine spray, an itch reliever and SPF 15 sun screen.

*   *   *

*   *   *

After the trading session, we were taken to the Huitoto village. On the way, we passed the local general store with its thatched roof. It had 1 X 10 board siding painted bright blue and a corrugated tin awning. The windows had no screens but did have wooden shutters. The street in front of the store was dirt but had been graded to provide drainage along the edges but there was no tractor or any other vehicle in sight. A sign in Spanish advertised cerveza (beer), gaseosa (sodas) and curichi (snacks). Near the store were several children dressed in conventional shirts or T-shirts and shorts or jeans. The one adult male was shirtless, slightly potbellied and wearing shorts. At least two pre-teen girls were carrying big, healthy looking babies around. They all looked healthy.

We walked across a field of grass used to pasture carabou and for soccer games. The field covered about ten acres. There were no mosquitoes but chiggers were present. DEET on the ankles and socks worked well to prevent chiggers.

General Store

On a bluff above the Apayacu River
A few miles from the Amazon
Sits a lone general store.

Bright blue planks and a thatch roof,
A corrugated tin awning and no window screens
They sell cerveza, gaseosa and curichi
But no chocolates.

*   *   *

In the village of the Huitoto, we entered similar thatched meeting hall for an exhibition of their native songs and dances. The Bora and Huitoto alternated in holding the dances and craft sales.

The Huitoto native dress was of the same material as that of the Bora. Men wore the loin cloth but the females wore sleeveless dresses that extended half way down the thigh. Their tapa clothing had a fringe and the decoration consisted of geometric figured stripes and edging. The women had painted ankle and wrist bands of white with brown trim. The men were had white dots in a curving line on each side of the chest from shoulder to hip. Several of the men had scars in the same pattern instead of the white dots. Both men and women wore head bands of tapa cloth and feathers except one man who had a snake skin that trailed down his back.

One old woman had moved with the tribe from the Putumayo River area of Columbia when she was six. At seventy, she was still very active and right in the middle of the dancing exhibition.

The Huitoto had some trade goods but their primary concern was demonstrating crafts and the folk dances. They sang and danced three dances for us. One dance was about a turtle. Another was about an anaconda and involved stepping in a springy log about thirty feet long. The third dance was neither announced nor discussed but looked and sounded much like the others.

After the demonstration, we started back down the dirt road toward the field. A turn off the road lead to an incline studded with logs leading down to the river. Near the bottom of this cord road was a large house on stilts. This was probably the main landing during high water. Several little boys were playing in boats tied to the shore. A covered log raft was loaded with sawed lumber was tied to the shore nearby.

*   *   *

We boarded the Rio Amazonas and sailed on down the Apayacu for a couple miles. The next stop was for a trip into the jungle. There was a house at the boat landing in which an Indian woman of indeterminate age was preparing supper. She was asked about preparing manioc and demonstrated how to peel and prepare it for cooking.

The jungle trip began with a short walk through a field that was going back to the jungle. Bananas and two kinds of ginger were relicts of man's activity. Several other dooryard plants were also visible but would soon be crowded out by native growth.

At the edge of the jungle we saw the flower and seed of the Amazon Lily (Eucharis grandiflora) and many of the plants found in plant shops as specimen plants—Marantas, Calatheas, Heliconia, Miconia, ariods like Diffenbachia, etc.

A convoy of leaf-cutter ants was speeding along a vine with large pieces of leaf to transport back to their nest hanging above high water.

167

Leafcutter Ants

Half inch ants in tandem
at half inch intervals
each with a large leaf umbrella
their life is never dull.
Down a branch to the trees trunk
onto a wavering vine to a nest on a limb
they shred the leaves and add fungi
and tend their gardens above high water.

*   *   *

A large nest of very touchy ants was hanging from a limb near the trail. A group of plastic looking, tough textured, salmon colored cup fungi were growing out of decaying vegetation on the jungle floor. A termite nest surrounded a tree trunk about ten feet above the ground. One tree supported a population of mean ants that lived in the plant's hollow spines. These ants kept the tree and the ground around its base free of competition from other terrestrial plants, parasitic plants and insect pests.

We encountered an army ant trail by stepping in it. Several people received painful bites. The trail was several inches wide and disappeared into the jungle in both directions.

Army Ants

I had heard stories of Army Ants
Charging through the jungle
Devouring everything in their path.

A gross exaggeration
But the are vicious.
A three inch trail disappears
Into the jungle in a few feet both ways.

A misstep on the trail
Resulted in three quick bites
And quick forays by the ants
To see if there were anything to eat.

*   *   *

A vine grew with spiral form of leaf growth to prevent shading its own leaves. A plant called the Upside Down Tree was a screw pine. It had more bulk in its spiny buttress roots than in the vegetative growth that extended twenty feet into the air.

This was where I spotted a small black and red lizard; and we captured a Dead-Leaf Toad that looked like a dead leaf. I was disappointed at the lack of butterflies but it may have been the wrong season.

Jungle Drinking Water

Most natives drink directly from the Amazon
Instead of boiling or filtering the water.
Then they drink some juice of the ficus tree
Twice a year as a purgative just like they ought to
To kill the internal parasites from the river.
No tea or fuel to boil the water.

*   *   *

Bedar showed us a ficus tree whose buttressed trunk was twenty five feet across at ground level. This tree's poisonous sap was used by the natives to purge the internal parasites accumulated from drinking the raw river water. About once or twice a year, everyone takes the cure rather than boil the water. He also showed us a plant that was supposed to cure snake bite. He claimed his father had been zapped by a Fer-de-lance and lived thanks to this plant.

We finally entered another recently abandoned field that was grown over with swordgrass. As we passed a big breadfruit tree a chorus of frogs piped our way into the clearing near where the boat was moored.

*   *   *

We sailed down the Amazon past the major town of *Pevas* where we turned back upstream and docked for a customs check. While we waited for the local authority, we watched a herd of carabou on the mud flat. Cattle egrets were eating ticks, etc., off of them.

While we waited, a local ferry pulled in for their customs check. This was two hulls fastened together with one engine. The deck was covered but otherwise opens to the elements. Hammocks were hung and people were in them or on the deck. A woman came back to the stern and pulled up a bucket of water from the river. She poured this over her head and down inside her dress. Then she combed her hair and was ready to go ashore.

A canoe with two women and a large pot paddled up to the stern port quarter of the ferry. The pot contained soup which was sold by the bowl. A single plastic bowl was rinsed in the river and refilled for the next customer. One of the women noticed the boat was taking on water. She used the bowl to bail out the boat before filling it for the next customer.

Pevas Fast Food

We stopped at Ft Pevas on the Amazon
For a passport check.
I watched a local ferry with people sleeping
In hammocks and on the crowded deck.

A dugout pulled up beside the ferry
Two women and a pot of stew
The stew was sold from a single bowl
Rinsed in the Amazon just for you.

One woman noticed the dugout
Was taking on a little water.
She used the bowl to bail it out
Before serving the next customer.

*　　*　　*

Finally, a young Peruvian Army captain, complete with sword, came down from the compound accompanied by three men in flight suits.

They boarded and inspected the documents and walked around the ship. After the official inspection was over, there was a little time for socializing. The ones in flight suits were two officers and a sergeant from a helicopter squadron of Hueys that supported this and the other river forts. They had trained with the US Navy.

*   *   *

Leaving the check point we backed into the main stream of the Amazon and stopped at a river camp near the *Yana Yacu River.*

After supper, we went out to hunt caiman. Two boats went out. Our boat spotted a pair of red eyes but they disappeared before we got close. The mosquitoes were not out in force and did not bother unless we were close to the shore. A few minutes later, we spotted another pair of eyes. The boat drove into the cane along the shore. Bader grabbed and came up with a caiman about four feet long. We looked at it and shot pictures. Then, we showed it to the other boat and released it back to the river. One good point about the caiman is that it controls the Piranha population.

On the return trip we made a detour up a small stream to sit for a few minutes and listen to the jungle. Several species of frogs and toads were calling, and several night birds added unique punctuations to the stillness. We bumped a patch of water lettuce in the dark. It lit up with hundreds of fluorescent spots of cold blue light.

Several species of fireflies were blinking ancestral coded messages to potential mates. I asked Bader if he had ever called fireflies. He said he had never heard of doing that so I explained the process. With a little practice he could be the most popular firefly on the river.

*   *   *

15 June. Farther Down the Amazon

It was overcast and barely light. The entire group was up and ready at 0600 for trip to see the Victoria Regina water lilies. This lily is the largest floating plant in the world. The buoyant, circular leaves can support up to twenty pounds. Its stark white blossoms are more than a foot across and weigh several pounds. Growing in many botanical gardens and private lily ponds, the Victoria Regina occurs naturally in backwater ponds along the upper Amazon.

Our two aluminum boats raced over small waves and through flotillas of water lettuce (<u>Pistia</u> <u>stratiotes</u>) and rafts of water hyacinth (<u>Eichornia</u> <u>crassipes</u>). Of the three species of water hyacinths along the Amazon, this species has violet flowers with a distinctive yellow spot on a bluish field and inflated leaf petioles. Large trees, with a satellite mass of plant material, floated like small islands. They were a menace to navigation.

CROSSING THE AMAZON

The John boat bounced over a low chop
Storm clouds spawned rain in the distance
The sunshine had stopped
The water was grey-brown and 18 miles wide
After a 30 foot winter drop
No land in sight but rafts of hyacinths and pistia
And trees with epiphytes hanging sideways
In their tops

*   *   *

The sun was late in appearing. It was hiding behind a cloud bank that was spawning rain showers in the distance. We were fortunate that none of the showers was in our path. Thin patches of blue stained the uneven white-gray stratus clouds.

*   *   *

The camcorder decided its internal humidity was too great and would not work. Keeping it in our cool stateroom caused condensate and a malfunction. It had to warm up and dry out before it would work properly. It was kept in the engine room at outside temperature to avoid this problem.

*   *   *

We beached the boats on the mud and climbed a steep, six-foot alluvial berm up to the mud flat. A prostrate water primrose (Jussiaea sp?) was sprouting and spreading on the mud surface. It would become one of the dominant plants on the mud flat. Myriads of young toads the size of a nickel were roaming the mud flat consuming gnats and blackflies. Again, it was surprising that mosquitoes were not a problem.

Rice had been broadcast on the mud flat. This field (?) covered about fifty acres. Sowing rice by broadcasting the seed on the mud as the water recedes differs from the Asian process of sprouting and sprigging rice in paddies. Along the Amazon, no water management is available and paddy culture would be near impossible. There is a scarcity of labor and machinery and seasonal changes of the water level along the Amazon may be thirty feet or more.

We followed a path across the rice field to avoid trampling any more rice than necessary. The field got muddier as we went until we stopped on a high spot near a pond. These backwater ponds are locally called "igarapes". Bedar waded out barefooted and cut a lily flower and a section of leaf and stem.

The flower bud was beginning to open with several large white petals unfurled. The bud was the size of a quart jar. It was a pinkish hue on the outside or underside of the petals. The stem was an inch in diameter and covered with sharp, half-inch long spines. The leaf top was flat and green and about four to five foot in diameter with an upturned rim about two inches high. The underside of the leaf was reddish purple. Modified veins of the leaf were flattened vertically forming flotation compartments on the bottom of the leaf. The veins and ribs were covered with spines. Many pinhead size white eggs of something were attached to the base of the spines. The leaf petiole or stem was up to twenty feet long which allowed the leaf to float when the river rose. These plants have few enemies except the manatee that does not seem to mind the prickles.

On the pond was a young man standing in his dugout canoe spearing fish. He had three carp-like fish with a total live weight of about five pounds. He offered them for sale and they were purchased for lunch.

*   *   *

Back on the Rio Amazonas, we had just finished breakfast when porpoise began breaking water. We were near the confluence where the Rio Atacuari emptied its dark organic water into the chocolate brown Amazon. Peru was on the west bank and Columbia was on the east. Individual porpoise were pink, pink and gray or all gray. The popular theory was that these dolphins were stranded almost a thousand miles up stream from the Pacific in what became the upper Amazon about 70 million years ago when the Andes rose. The porpoise and several other relict marine or estuarine species currently found in the upper Amazon adapted to fresh water and the food supply on the river. I never did get a good picture of them.

*   *   *

After lunch, we prepared to go fishing for Piranha. We each had a hand line with a small weight and a strong foot-long wire leader attached to a half-inch hook. Each boat was supplied with a pound of raw meat cut into small chunks. The boats proceeded to a small backwater and tied up to some overhanging branches. Canoe paddles and tree branches were used to beat on the water surface to attract the Piranha. Then we baited our hooks and dropped them into the river. Everyone lost bait as small fish hit and ran.

It was difficult to get the bait down to where the larger fish were. I managed to catch two fish. One was what was locally called a red piranha and the other one a white piranha. These fish belong to a sub-family of predatory Disc Characins or the Characidae, called the Serrasalminae. They are high bodied, strongly compressed laterally and the belly is edged with saw-like toothed scales. They are ferocious carnivores. The most common genera are <u>Pygocentrus</u>, <u>*Rooseveltiella*</u> and <u>Serrasalmo</u>.

The red piranha appeared to be <u>Serrasalmo</u> <u>rhombeus</u> or spotted piranha. It has 16-19 dorsal rays, 31-36 anal rays, 30-33 tooth scales, a soft adipose fin and very small scales. Breeding colors are dull silver with many irregular gray spots. This fish can get to two feet long and live on shoals.

The white piranha was in the sharp-nosed piranha group possibly <u>Pygocentrus</u> <u>piraya</u>. It has 17-18 dorsal and 31-32 anal spines a shorter skull with a steeply arched forehead and overdeveloped protruding jaws. It is a blue-green with small light and darker dots. Each was about eight inches long. They both had protruding jaws with a number of sharp teeth. The dorsal and tail fins were ragged where pieces had been bitten out. This is a solitary fish attacking from ambush. It commonly feeds on fins of other fish

A total of fifteen piranha and a couple small catfish were caught. These were taken back to the ship and served for lunch.

Although they have a bad reputation, the piranha is not a major problem. They do not attack large warm-blooded animals so swimming with them is not dangerous. Caiman, river otters, catfish and larger piranha usually keep the populations in check. The river is even safe for swimming so long as there is no blood and thrashing of the water.

*   *   *

Later in the day, we entered the *Caballo Cocha River*. We passed the town of *Caballo Cocha* and entered into Lake Caballo Cocha. When the ship turned around and went back to dock at Caballo Cocha, we loaded up the small boats went up the Rio Palo Seco to look for sloth and other wildlife.

On the trip up stream, we were hailed from the bank by a woman with three children. She wanted to show Bedar a bird that looked much like an owl from a distance. On inspection, it was a Greater Potoo (<u>Nyctibius</u> <u>grandis</u>). It belongs to the Camprimulgidae family along with the goatsuckers and nighthawks. The bird was well equipped for night flying with large eyes and a large gaping mouth to scoop up flying insects. It had been killed by her husband with a shotgun. They would either sell it to us or have it for supper. We did not buy it.

There was a Brazil- or Para-nut tree (<u>Berthollrtia</u> <u>excelsa</u>) where we pulled in. This tree was smooth barked for about forty feet. The pod of nuts was about 6 inches in diameter with a hard thick wall. It weighted about a kilo containing 18-24 triangular 2 inch nuts.

We saw several pairs of parrots in the tree tops and many Jacana on the mud flats. A large raft of water hyacinths was partially floating and partially stranded on the mud. This was something I had wanted to see in its native habitat. However, we saw no sloth and no snakes.

On the way back, the driver and I both spotted a sloth high in a <u>Cecropia</u> tree. We disturbed his beauty sleep by bumping the tree. Over the course of several minutes, he climbed higher into even smaller branches. By the way, the sloth is one of the favorite foods of the Jaguar.

*   *   *

The boats stopped at the landing at the foot of the main street of the town of Caballo Cocha. It was a town of maybe 1000 people. It had a square with a war memorial. At one end of the square were the Catholic Church and the municipal building was at the other end. A general store, several bars, at least two small restaurants, two pantadaria or bakeries occupied the remaining sides of the square. Along the road to the mooring were several upper class homes. Several public housing complexes made of cast concrete were located just off the square. A community power plant produced electricity which was available to the street lights and houses four hours a night. We could hear radios and see the flashing light of TVs playing in some of the houses.

The general store stocked sodas, beer, and a few necessities but there was neither much variety nor supply. No chocolate or even cookies.

All the kids wanted to look through binoculars and cameras. Some wore thongs but most were barefoot. One young lady had glasses.

Some of the young teen males did not appear to like tourists in general. They were dressed in modish clothing, at least, for the village and they hung out together like teens everywhere.

Several old men had large open wounds on the face that looked like leishmanisis. There were, also, a two blind people sitting in the square.

Caballo Cocha

A major trading point on Rio Caballo Cocha
500 people and electricity four hours a day.
Two pantaderias and a general store
But no chocolate.

Most of the kids were barefoot
And wanted to look through the binoculars
And see themselves on the camcorder.
Typical kids.

Several teens in modish dress
Hanging out together
Avoiding us tourists.
How you gonna keep them up the Amazon?

Old men, blind or with leshmanisis
Sat in the square in the setting sun.

*　　*　　*

We made our way back to the ship and left the dock as the sun set. Mosquitos of several species came out of the tall grass along the river.

We had supper and watched the National Geographic special on the lower Amazon as we sailed down the *Rio Caballo Cocha* back to the Amazon.

*　　*　　*

16 June. Offload at Leticia and Back to Lima

We awoke early and found the Rio Amazonas tied to the southern (Peruvian) shore of the Amazon. The city of *Leticia, Colombia*, lay across the river. We finished packing and took the bags to the lounge. Breakfast was served, and we said farewell to the crew. I left my copy of Ridgley's *"A Guide to the Birds of Panama"* with Bedar. He did not have a copy, and I could get another copy if necessary.

While waiting for the boats to shuttle us to *Leticia*, I noticed that we had passed through a termite swarm during the night. Hundreds of conenose termites were running around on the deck. On closer inspection, these were a number of queens being followed closely by one or more males. It looked like little convoys of eighteen-wheelers. I asked Bedar if he had seen this before. He had seen termite swarms but did not recognize the significance. I briefly explained the life cycle of the termite to add to his store of knowledge.

Termite Swarm

An Amazon conenose termite swarm
Filled the night sky.
At dawn they had shed their wings
And the larger queens ran about
With several males following
Like a convoy of 18 wheelers

*   *   *

We boarded the aluminum boats for the last time for the trip to *Leticia* and *Tabatinga*, Brazil. The baggage would come on a later trip.

As we were pulling away from the Rio Amazonas, I watched the crew take all the garbage from the trip and throw it into the river.

Counterpoint

After three days of environmental saturation
We left the M/V Rio Amazonas
At Leticia Columbia.
From our ferry crossing the Amazon
We watched the crew
Dump our refuse into the Amazon.

*   *   *

It took half an hour to cover the three miles across the river. We disembarked and waited until the luggage showed up. We identified each of our bags and loaded the bags on three vehicles for transportation to the Rio Amazonas' office in *Leticia*.

A fuel truck was parked nearby. It was a primitive arrangement of a valve and a hose from the bottom of the tank. This probably resulted in the customer getting all the condensate and muck that settled out of the fuel. A sight valve consisted of an open Tygon tube from a fitting in the bottom of the tank tied to the top of the tank by a piece of wire.

A Colombian gunboat was moored to the dock. Armament was two .30 cal machine guns and what looked like a 20mm gun all covered with canvas. We passed the ship and continued along a one-lane asphalt road to town. The billets of the local militia and the Columbian officers club faced this road.

Just as we entered town from the port road, a new Bronco stalled on the corner. The four jock-types in the vehicle gave us a good looking over complete with pictures. The vehicle magically started and disappeared. I don't know whose files we are in, but we're on somebody's list.

*   *   *

We left our hand baggage at the Rio Amazonas office on the Plaza de Armas and took a walking tour of *Leticia*. The shuttle bus to the *Tabatinga* airport would leave in about two hours. We wandered around town with no Colombian money. The moneychangers really did not want Intes and were offering only half of the official exchange rate. Where are the black marketers when you need them? We did not want to cash even a $20 traveler's check for a pile of Colombian money just for Cokes. I finally found Cokes at the hotel bar for one US dollar each.

Leticia probably contained about 5000 inhabitants. It was cleaner than its Peruvian counterparts. I guess this was because of the availability of money. It was a little after 0900 and there was little of interest in the few shops that were open. A toyshop selling European metal model cars and trucks was overpriced. Indian crafts were scarce, and the items available were very poor quality, very expensive or both. I had expected to find gem stones and was surprised to find only some geodes and some pink quartz.

The Colombian city of *Leticia* exists as a historical footnote. Prior to 1930, it belonged to Peru. By several international treaties, the Amazon was designated as an international waterway. Colombia did not have a port on the Amazon. The river was only twenty miles away from the rubber producing areas of southwestern Colombia. The presidents of Peru and Colombia got together in 1922 and arranged for transfer of Leticia to Columbia to take place in 1930. But, by 1930, there had been a revolution and the old president, Leguia, was overthrown. A half-breed soldier, Sanchez Cerro, had claimed the presidency. He changed his mind and re-annexed Leticia without notifying Colombia so Colombia declared war.

Cerro was murdered in 1933. During that three-year interval, Colombia bought several WWI warships, declared an unofficial war on Peru and blockaded the Amazon. The fleet was based at *Tarapaca* on the *Rio Putumayo* about 500 miles north of Leticia. The dispute went on including an attempt to take Iquitos. The League of Nations finally decided this foolishness had gone on long enough. After Cerro died, an international commission was sent to Leticia for a meeting with the two countries. The matter was settled in 1933, and Leticia became part of Colombia.

A monument in the Plaza de Armas located Leticia at 4 degrees 13 minutes south Latitude and 69 degrees 8 minutes west latitude. Elevation was 96 meters (316 feet). Average temperature was 27 degrees Celsius (78 degrees F). Rainfall averaged 2731 mm (175 in.). The average relative humidity was 84.4 percent.

*   *   *

Transportation to the airport arrived. People and bags were loaded on two old VW vans for the ride across the border to *Tabatinga*, Brazil. There was no customs' check to mark the border. Like Iquitos, everything came in by river or air. However, the existence of the border was plain. Roads and architecture went from bad to worse when we crossed into Brazil.

Tabatinga had existed as a military town with a joint-use airport since WWII. The civilian population had little in the way of luxuries. Many of the buildings along the way were concrete block painted apple green, fuchsia or some other bright (?), gaudy (?), gay (?) color. There were groups of people listening to the World Cup soccer game on radios turned up as high as possible.

The van swayed dodging potholes along what was supposed to be a two lane road. The Brazilian government was and, probably still is, building a new concrete, four lane divided highway from *Leticia* to the airport. Only about half of one half of one side was finished, and we drove on smooth concrete for less than a mile. The driver said this much construction had taken eight years so far. There was no evidence of equipment or recent construction. Once on the concrete, there was no way off until we reached the end. There was a drop-off of a foot or more on either side of the concrete.

The airport terminal building was old but serviceable. It looked like a WWII US military hanger. There were a few seats and a snack bar but no shops. Customs was primarily a passport check to make sure visas had been purchased. The requirement for yellow fever shots was ignored since they did not look at the shot records.

The World Cup soccer finals were on TV. Brazil was one of the contestants so the flight was delayed until after the game was completed. Most of the passengers and, probably, the crew appeared to be more willing to miss the flight than the end of the game.

For some reason, there were several people in Red Cross T-shirts and several Brazilian Army troops on duty at the airport. I guess they take soccer seriously.

*   *   *

A boy about eight years old was mixing with the crowd. He was outstanding because he had a marmoset sitting on his head or shoulder. The marmoset had a string tied around its waist that the boy held in his hand.

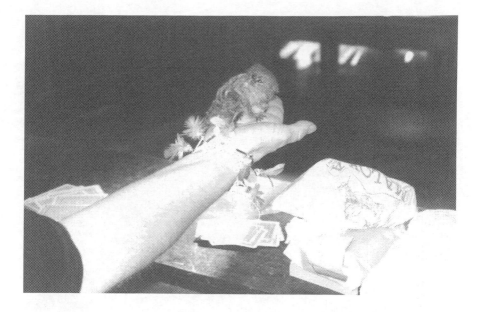

After customs, we were herded into the waiting area. If the terminal was Spartan then the international waiting room was a stoics' dream. There was barely standing room, no lights except the dirty windows and not even a drinking fountain. There were no smokers or it would not have been tolerable.

The Brazillian Varig airliner was cleaner and better appointed than even Aeroperu's international route planes. The cabin crew was also a couple quantum steps above the Aeroperu crews. They looked and acted much more professional.

We flew over the jungle in the daylight. The slash and burn farmsteads were clearly visible. The jungle was reclaiming many of the areas. I could not get to a window to shoot video and only managed a couple of still shots.

* * *

We arrived at Iquitos an hour late. This, however, made little difference since our Aeroperu flight to Lima had not left from Lima yet. The flight was to be delayed at least six hours. We were taken into town to the Rio Amazonas office to wait. We had missed lunch so the first item on our agenda was lunch. We checked our bags and were off to the Maloka restaurant for lunch and more shopping.

Lunch was very enjoyable. We sat on a veranda overlooking the Amazon. I had *Piacayu* (the largest, bony fresh water fish known) with manioc and plantains, a papaya, a Coke, an Incacola and a lemonade. I had not realized how dehydrated I had become. Carol had steak but the rest was the same.

The colonel and his wife from New Orleans joined us about half way through our lunch. We discussed the trip and watched a rain cloud drift across the river leaving a beautiful rainbow behind.

Some Japanese tourists were feeding a couple of monkeys in a big cage on the restaurants veranda. The monkeys were offered edible food like banana and inedible items like a slice of lime. The monkeys were smarter than you might think. They learned fast which ones fed them and who tried to fool them.

As we left the Maloka, we spotted a four-foot long green iguana on a limb next to the veranda. Looking carefully, we spotted four more of the lizards in various parts of the tree. The first one we saw was a large male that displayed beautifully several times before slowly disappearing into the leaves near the end of a branch. Another large iguana was higher and less visible. The other three were 18-24 inch juveniles. We shot a lot of pictures of them with the Amazon in the background.

The Rio Amazonas gift shop was open when we returned from lunch. Jewelry made from scales of the *Piacayu* fish, wooden bowls and dolphin carvings, blow guns, Indian paintings and such were for sale. Our group almost bought out their inventory.

* * *

Finally, our luggage and tickets were taken out to the airport. As we were waiting, Carol played solitaire while I watched the people and traffic passing in front of the office. A *raspa* salesman passed. A truck stopped to off-load several blocks of ice to deliver somewhere nearby. A young girl selling sliced oranges and watermelon stopped in and tried to make a sale.

One young man came in and offered to sell us a marmoset for one US dollar. The marmoset looked like it was barely weaned and would probably starve. The salesman insisted that we could stick it in a pocket, and it would be in fine shape when we got it to America. The poor little thing would not survive the cold drafts and the altitude changes of the airplane trip even if it were healthy. There is also six-month quarantine in Miami at the owner's expense. We told him, "Thank you, but no thanks."

The center of the Plaza de Armas was occupied by a fountain with a statue of the pink dolphin in its center. The fountain no longer works but the life size dolphin remained a landmark. I asked about the significance of the pink dolphin and this statue in particular. No one seemed to know except that the dolphin was the symbol of the city. On one side of the square was the "Iron House" designed and built by Dr Eiffel for the Great Exhibition in Paris for the turn of the century. It was bought, disassembled and moved to Iquitos by one of the rich rubber barons.

About 6 PM, we left the Rio Amazonas office for the airport. The sun was setting, and the jungle sounds were just beginning.

Aeroperu was ready about 8 and arrived in Lima at 9:40. A short uneventful ride to the Sheraton allowed us to check in by 11 PM for another short, high priced night in Lima.

Our Amazon adventure was over. On to Buenos Aires.

*   *   *

17 June. Lima to Buenos Aires

We were up at 5 AM. We packed and were ready for our ride to the airport through the early dawn. There had been one of the rare showers in Lima, and the atmosphere was heavier than usual. The omnipresent dust had become a thin, slippery coating on everything.

We were surprised to find that the Aeroperu flight to Santiago and Buenos Aires was on time. Customs was no trouble this time. They briefly looked in the bags and strapped a yellow plastic band around each bag. The waiting and luggage identification were the same as before.

The flight to Chile was almost dull. We jumped into the clouds and stayed out over the cold Pacific until we began to let down for the short stop in Santiago. The approach was over undeveloped, mountainous land and terminated at a joint-use military airfield. Our plane did not taxi close enough to the military side to get a good look at the Chilean Air Force. However, several C-130s were visible in the distance.

Santiago was built near the geographical center of Chile. It was established in 1541 by the conquistador, Pedro de Valdiva. He had been sent by Pizarro to explore and colonize Chile. Valdiva left Cuzco in January, 1540. A year later, after crossing the high, dry desert of northern Chile, he discovered the Central Valley. Here, he traced out the main streets and sited the major buildings of Santiago. Over the next twelve years, he explored and colonized Chile in spite of the constant harassment of the *Araucanian Indians*. The leader of the *Araucanians*, Lautaro, had learned to raise and handle horses and devised several strategies to defeat the Spanish cavalry. Valdiva was captured by the Araucanians in 1554 and executed. This protracted war became the theme of an epic poem, *La Araucana*, written by a Spanish officer, Alonso de Ercilla in the 1560s. It has been a rallying point ever since.

About 50 passengers deplaned in Chile, and about the same number boarded for the trip to Buenos Aires. We were not allowed to leave the plane. We did not have a visa for Chile and, with the recent political climate in Chile, I was not too disappointed.

*   *   *

After an hours' stop, we were in the air again.

Takeoff was about 5 PM. We headed east, out of the sun and clouds. The snow on Andes was beautiful in the late afternoon sun.

We were out of the mountains and Chile in a few minutes, since Santiago was less than fifty miles from the Argentine border. Our track lead out over a land of low hills. They ran parallel to the mountains like ripples on a pond. To the south was the Rio San Juan Desaguadero that ran south. It had two reservoirs backed up by hydroelectric dams. A white ring around the lakes showed that they were about 20 feet below their normal water level. These lakes were located on the extreme western border of Argentina. The electricity generated by the dams probably serviced Santiago and eastern Chile, as well as the nearby cities of *Mercedes, Mendoza* and *San Luis* in western Argentina.

We flew steadily eastward into the gathering dusk. Although over the Argentine wine country, I saw no vineyards or any farming activity.

The hills gradually disappeared. Flat plains studded with playa lakes replaced the hills. All of the playas were dry. The area looked similar to the Texas Panhandle near Lubbock.

Several settlements came into sight and disappeared under the wing. These settlements were round groves of trees surrounding a series of buildings which, in turn, surrounded a central round corral. These settlements looked like they were associated with fields of winter grain. The fields had circular irrigation systems set in a grid of cross roads. This looked similar to grain fields in Kansas and eastern Colorado.

Sunlight disappeared, and the land changed beneath us. More trees and houses became visible on the plains as we approached Buenos Aires from the south. Orchards became common. Finally, we passed over a large residential area and landed.

*   *   *

The *Ezeiza Airport* was located about thirty miles south of Buenos Aires. Encroachment by housing areas must present a problem but it is not considered pressing in areas other than the U.S.

We deplaned into a large warehouse of a reception area and were processed through customs. Another wait and we found our luggage. I noticed my big folding bag had one outside pocket unzipped up to the yellow customs band. I checked and found my electric razor missing. There were no officials in sight to report this to, but both the airline and customs people said I should have reported the theft immediately. Our guide helped straighten this out, but I would have to report the loss to the Aeroperu office on Tuesday morning.

Our guide was a grey-haired German lady who was accompanied by a male German driver about the same age. We drove through the night on a modern freeway to downtown Buenos Aires and the hotel. The freeway was called the Pisia and was part of the original Pan-AM highway.

At the hotel an armed guard was in the lobby and a there was a guard near the elevator on each floor. Our room was on the fourth floor. It had lockable closets with a safe. There were bars on the windows backed up by a metal roll up window cover. The room was the most fortified place I'd slept in years. Some how all this security did not promote a sense of security.

*   *   *

Some background information on Argentina, in general, and Buenos Aires, in particular, is in order. The explorer, Juan Diaz de Solis, discovered the *Plata River* and estuary in 1516 and was killed by the Indians. The English explorer, Sebastian Cabot, entered the estuary in 1526 and built a fort. He found no gold or silver, and the Indians burned his fort so he returned to Spain. Emperor Charles V of Spain sent Pedro de Mendoza to the Plata in 1535 to build forts and find a route to Peru. Mendoza established a port city of *Santa Maria del Buen Aire* on the site of the present capitol. The town was surrounded by the local Indians and starved out. The town was finally evacuated in 1541. Argentina dates from 1553 with its first permanent settlers and spent its first 224 years under the Viceroy of Peru in Lima. The administrative center for Argentina was located at Santiago del Estero, then at Tucuman and, finally, at Cordoba. A new viceroyalty was erected in 1777 that ruled all of Argentina, Uruguay, Paraguay, and southern Bolivia from its new capitol at Buenos Aires.

A combination of regionalism, the vice regal tradition, authoritarianism, church-state power base and government fraud and favoritism made independence a difficult goal. In 1806/7, England invaded Argentina and was repulsed. An epic poem entitled "The Argentine Victory" gave the term "Argentine" prominence and the first hint of unity. In 1808, Napoleon invaded Spain, forced the abdication of the king and set his brother on the throne. Spanish America set up "caretaker" governments in the administrative centers. Argentina, at the *cabildo abierto* or town meeting, declared independence from Spain on 9 July, 1816.

A hero of Argentina, Jose de San Martin, led a force over the Andes to help the Chilean patriots drive out the Spanish royalists. San Martin was assisted by the Chilean navy under the direction of a renegade British admiral, Lord Cochrane. Political instability prevailed. Paraguay became independent in 1814, Bolivia in 1825 and Uruguay in 1828.

Bernardino Rivadavia tried to unite and Europeanize the country beginning in 1820 but was overthrown in 1826 by Juan Manuel de Rosas. Rosas, the son of a Buenos Aires patrician, instigated a Creole revolt in Buenos Aires. He gradually took over the entire country since the country preferred order to liberty. With a strong-arm gang called the *Mazorca*, his dictatorship lasted until 1852. His army, under General Justo Jose de Urquiza, revolted and, assisted by an invasion from Brazil and Uruguay, Rosas was deposed.

A new constitution, adopted in 1853, was based on the Constitution of the United States. Another 20 years of internal conflict tired and, finally, stabilized the government, and Buenos Aires become a kind of federal district. This, and the opening of the pampas by the crushing defeat of the Indians by General Julio A. Roca in 1879, resulted in relative peace until 1916.

Social change was initiated by the rapid economic development in the second half of the nineteenth century, the rise of the urban middle class and the depression of 1890. The Radical Party was founded as an opposition party but the conservative oligarchy remained in power. A member of the oligarchy, Roque Saenz Pena pushed through reforms including the Electoral Law. This change permitted the first elected president in 1912. The first elected Radical president was Hipolito Irigoyen.

Irigoyen, described as "muddleheaded" and "as autocratic as any caudillo", made some social changes. Minimum wages, maximum working hours, etc. were proposed. But the president meddled in provincial affairs, showed no respect for Congress and, gradually, appointed a group of corrupt friends to administrative posts. By 1930, it was evident that he could not deal with the effects of a world-wide depression. There was no serious opposition to a military coup d',tat on September 4, 1930.

General Jose E. Uriburu, believing the Army's mission was to regenerate the nation, had led the coup. But Uriburu's dictatorship lasted only about a year. He was overthrown by General Agustin P. Justo, who believed in a nonpolitical Army.

General Justo won the called election in 1931 and ruled until 1938. Roberto Ortiz won the election in 1938 but resigned in 1940 because of diabetes. His vice-president, Ramon Castillo, became president. Castillo used the attack on Pearl Harbor as an excuse to declare near martial law in Argentina. Castillo was removed by the Army coup on June 4, 1943. This coup eventually leads to the rise to power of Juan Peron.

Colonel Juan D. Peron had served as military attaché to Italy during the term of Mussolini and had seen the importance of the trade unions, industrialization, nationalization and Five-Year Economic Plans, etc. To gain the support of the long neglected masses of the lower class and of the labor community, he knew he would have to help them improve their lot. As a party to the coup, Peron took the office of Secretary of Labor. From this position, he encouraged labor reforms and promoted unionization. He got money for public housing and legislation for compulsory paid holidays. A macho image was cultivated, and he became patron of athletes and entertainment stars and shared their glory. One special entertainer was Eva Duarte, a singer and radio personality.

He was arrested in 1945 but was freed as a result of a virtual revolution by the *descamisados*—the men in shirt-sleeves. He was released on October 17, 1945 and married Eva "Evita" Duarte. Peron did not take any office himself but did place his friends in key positions while he prepared for the election in February 1946. His supporters created a political party, the *Partido Laborista*, and Peron was nominated for president.

With the support of the Catholic Church and the labor unions, Peron won the presidency, most of the seats in the Chamber of Deputies and all but two seats in the Senate. He and Evita ruled and brought Argentina into the industrialized world. He broke the *estancieros* power but retained land values.

Evita died in 1952, and the regime deteriorated. Corruption, rising living costs, and other troubles led to a coup in September 1955. The provisional garrisons lead their troops against Buenos Aires, and the Navy blockaded the Plata. Peron took refuge on a Paraguayan gunboat and went into exile.

*   *   *

The military removed the Peronistas from the military, federal and state governments, judiciary and universities and put the trade unions under military *interventores*. Elections were called in 1958 but the Peronists were not allowed to nominate a candidate. A Radical, Arturo Frondizi, won with the help of the Peronists.

Frondizi allowed foreign oil leases, ordered a general wage increase and a general amnesty for political prisoners and allowed Peronistas to vote in the March 1962 elections. Many of the Peronistas won, and the military, under General Raul Poggi, deposed Frondizi and annulled the election results. Senate President Jose Maria Guido was sworn into office to prevent Poggi from becoming president and a new election was called for July 7, 1963.

Dr. Arturo Illia was elected president. He was indecisive and a weak president. He was removed from office by the military and General Ongania took over. And on it goes.

At the time of our trip, the city of Buenos Aires had a population of twelve million, over half the total population of Argentina. Population density for the country was roughly 16 per square mile. The ethnic composition was about 90 per cent white, 9 per cent mestizo, 1-2 percent Indian with a couple hundred Negroes. The figures are a little misleading since Argentina's liberal definition of white was anyone not obviously non-white.

*   *   *

Argentina never had much of a black population, and the Indians were effectively eliminated by General Roca, the "last of the conquistadores," in the pampas pacification campaign of 1879. For the next hundred years, immigrants from southern Europe populated the rural areas. This contributed to the whiteness of the population and the European or Creole culture of the country. This also accounts, in part, for the predominant 52 per cent of the population classified as middle class.

The large immigrant influx resulted in an integration problem. Many of the third and fourth-generation Germans, Italians, English and Spanish still think of themselves as Germans, Italians, English or Spanish. Like Californians, there are few native Argentines.

By popular Argentine definition, Creole means the Spanish cultural core modified by native Indian traditions. The primary symbol of the Creole culture was the gaucho or Argentine cowboy. He descended from the Indians that had taken the Spaniards horses when Buenos Aires was evacuated in 1541. He was a *mestizo* living on the plains on horseback chasing wild cattle and bad Indians. Gaucho traits like drinking mate (a native tea from Holley leaves) and eating *asado* (barbecued whole cow) are dying out except in literature. The *tango*, a Creole folk dance, still survives in the tango clubs of the Baja and in the movies. This is much like our own cowboys and Indians.

*   *   *

18 June. Buenos Aires

Buenos Aires is about 35 degrees south latitude and 58 degrees west longitude. San Antonio was about 6000 miles northwest at roughly 29 degrees north and 99 degrees west.

It was mid winter with the low temperature in the mid 30's and the high expected in the mid 50's. The sky was overcast and there was a brisk breeze.

We had breakfast in the hotel dining room. Our guide called to tell us that our tour of Buenos Aires was rescheduled for the afternoon and we had the morning free. They neglected to tell us that this was a national holiday, Flag Day, and that nothing was open. Our travel agent struck again.

After double locking the room, we checked the camcorder and other valuables in at the front desk and went for a walk. The downtown area of Buenos Aires was like most big cities as the city wakes up. Windows were full of merchandise and our hotel was in the gallery district with many art galleries. We headed over to the mall area in case anything would open and arrived as the doors opened. Most of the mall stores ignored the holiday and were open as usual.

We spent the morning in and out of a hundred shops. We looked a lot and only bought a few things. Carol bought a nice leather coat and we bought a leather bag and some jewelry and looked some more. Several of the shops had signs in English or signs that they spoke English. The signs in English were usually in Spanish word order and looked much like some of our one case Spanish. Some of the spoken English was American but most was high school. Those who spoke English were eager to practice.

Lunch was in one of the restaurants recommended by our guide. The owner had been in show business and there were pictures of him with many of the celebrities of WW II and postwar South America. Service was interminable. The menu consisted of several combinations of steak and fried potatoes. The choice was beef *frito* or *chorrizo*. The *frito* meant grilled steak. The *chorrizo* was not sausage as in Texas but a roast or grilled filet two inches thick. This was typical Argentine fare.

*   *   *

We returned to the hotel to go on our tour of the city. The tour group was mixed—six Japanese who spoke English, several Mexican citizens and us. We passed the cathedral which was closed, the Pink House or capitol, the treasury and the national bank. We crossed Avenida Libertador, the widest main street in the world (600 feet wide, 12 lanes with three wide, vegetated medians) and passed the statues of Jose de San Martin, Don Quixote and others.

The tour passed the port area. It was much like other ports around the world with a lot of warehouses, grain elevators and processing plants in various states of repair. The port itself and most of the ships were out of sight behind these buildings. The port was on the *Rio de la Plata* or Silver River. The *Plata* was known as the widest river in the world but there is debate whether the *Plata* is, indeed, a river and not an estuary. The *Parana* and *Uruguay Rivers* come together and enter the *Plata* about 50 miles north of Buenos Aires where Argentina and Uruguay meet on the Argentine border. These rivers and the largest railway system in Latin America transported wheat and sugar from *the Chaco* to the north, and wine from *Mendoza* to the west. Beef, mutton, leather and wool came from the Patagonia. Sugar from *Tucuman* and linseed oil from *Entre Rios* and *Corrientes* came to Buenos Aires for shipment to Europe.

The ferry terminal offered a three hour conventional ferry ride or ninety minute hydrofoil service to Montevideo, Uruguay. Montevideo was a hundred miles to the east on the north side of the Rio Plata.

The tour then entered the Boca area. The Boca area was low lying swampy beach near the port where many WWI immigrants from Italy settled. Argentina did nothing to support these invisible settlers until they tried to claim it as an independent country. The houses were built cheaply of concrete blocks. The structures were painted bright colors reminiscent of the voodoo or *santero* cultures. The *Tango*, as an international symbol for Argentina was originated in this part of town and several Tango clubs advertised nightclub acts of *Tango* and other Latin dances. One of Argentina's outstanding artists was born and raised in Boca and much of his money went to improve the lot of the Boca people.

The tour passed the largest shopping mall in Argentina. Then on to one of the city park where most of the people of Buenos Aires seemed to be on this holiday afternoon. We passed several large art museums and galleries, all of which were closed for the day.

*　　*　　*

On return to the hotel, we thought we had a choice of a tour of the tango clubs or going out for a good meal. We found that the Tango tours were all booked. The concierge made reservations for us at a five star Argentine restaurant, the Au Bin Fin, for some authentic Argentine food. We dressed for dinner and had the doorman hail a taxi and give the driver instructions on how to get there.

I don't know what the instructions were but it cost about ten dollars get there and only about two dollars to get back. Looking on a map the next day we only went about ten blocks from the hotel.

The restaurant was a former upper class home. The dining rooms were the house's rooms and still decorated with imported fabric wall coverings, fire places, art and tapestries of the 1890s. The menu was continental haute cuisine and mostly French. The meal, wine list and service was outstanding but nothing memorable.

The Argentines we had seen so far did not seem to be a happy people. There was no laughing or joking in the mall or the restaurants. Everyone seemed serious. As one author said they looked back to the happier times in the early twentieth century when Argentina was neither poor nor misgoverned. They did not want to face the present and no leadership or plan how to prepare for the future. Anti-Peronists, including the military whom Peron had used, the upper class from whom much had been taken and the middle class that had been wrecked by megainflation, said it was Peron's fault. Labor and the lower classes, for whom Peron had robbed the upper and middle classes, said it was the fault of the anti-Peronist coalition that had failed to solve the problems after removing Peron.

Back at the hotel, we spent a couple hours sorting and packing for the return trip to Lima the next afternoon.

*   *   *

19 June. Buenos Aires and Return to Lima

The morning air was cool—in the 40's. It was 0900 and time for a walk. We had breakfasted at the hotel, finished packing and checked the baggage with the concierge until plane time. Our appointment with the Aeroperu airline office was at 1000 to settle the claim of my stolen razor.

We walked the eight blocks to the Aeorperu office and spent another twenty minutes window shopping. The office opened and we were directed to see a young lady that spoke fair English. We explained our case. She said she could only give us one kilo credit or roughly ten US dollars. However, if we would see the office in Miami, we could surely settle for the entire amount. This sounded like a brush-off but there was not use arguing. The Pissarro's idiot children's airline was not concerned that their employees were accused of theft or about the sloppy security of Peruvian customs or the international airport. I really did not understand their position. When we returned to San Antonio and contacted Aeroperu in Miami they did not answer the mail and we never heard from them.

We spent the rest of the morning window shopping and visited several art galleries and antique dealers. There are some outstanding young Argentine artists, most of which live in Europe or elsewhere. They send some of their work back home to Argentina for sale. Buenos Aires has had a long reputation as a home for the arts in Latin America.

The galleries had many old European works in marble, bronze, porcelain and oil. Most of the work was Spanish or Italian and I did not recognize any of the artists.

Very few of the antiques were of *gaucho* or *creole* origin. There were a few spur rowels and a few fancy silver sheathed knives and *mat'e* sets of questionable authenticity. Toys of the 40's and 50's were at a premium. Turn of the century lamps, marble mantels and glassware and Ching Dynasty porcelain were common items.

Typical souvenirs of Argentina were bolas, gaucho capes and hats, and replica mat'e cups and daggers. These were priced beyond the range of casual souvenirs with prices of 30-150 US dollars. Best buys were leather goods such as coats, skirts, handbags and luggage.

I asked in one shop that had minerals in the window if they had Argentine mineral specimens or fossils. The clerks had no knowledge other than the stuff was for sale at the marked price. There were trilobites and fish from Wyoming, geodes from Brazil, amber from the Baltic and shells from the Philippines but nothing from Argentina.

* * *

We had lunch at one of the popular restaurants. It had the air of a working class downtown eatery that turned over the crowd as fast as possible. The menu was various meat dishes with fried potatoes. Since we had fried steak the previous day, we tried *chorizo*. This turned out to be an inch-thick grilled filet instead of thin frying steaks. Thick sliced fried potatoes came with the meal and I saw no other vegetable available. One person was eating what looked like fish but I did not recognize it on the menu. There was a choice of Coke, Fanta orange or coffee for drinks.

We found no place served the national beverage, mat'e. Mat'e is a tea made from the leaf of a holly tree. I asked in several places and at the hotel. Our guide said it might be found in a few places but it was not popular. I did not even see packaged mat'e for sale. Hot chocolate, however, was popular. It was served with a kind of chocolate cookie called a *churo*.

* * *

Back at the hotel, we paid our bill and gathered up the luggage shortly before transportation arrived. The driver was the same old German that had picked us up at the airport. Our guide, however, was a young Argentine lady who spoke English with a Spanish accent.

On the way to the airport, we discussed our stay in Argentina. One subject of particular interest was inflation. Our guide said that she had received her paycheck one Friday when the government decided to devalue the currency by one thousand to one. This meant that on Saturday her week's check would not buy bus fare. People were allowed to withdraw and convert one hundred new dollars per week per family. People literally starved and died because of lack of medicine. Actually what happened was what the government called "pisification". The government converted all funds to Argentine pesos at 75% devaluation. A $100 US suddenly became 23 pesos.

The Argentine inflation rate was about 400 per cent per year at the time we were there. Peru's inflation rate was 1600 per cent and Brazil's 3000 per cent.

We were cruising along on the inside lane of the freeway towards the airport when a truck broke down in the outer lane and a car cut in front of us. Our driver tried to stop but hit the car. Both vehicles pulled off the road and the drivers traded information. No one was hurt and neither vehicle was badly damaged. We were back on the road in about fifteen minutes. The driver said he had not had an accident in twenty five years. He said he could have avoided hitting the car but if he had hit the brakes, a truck behind us would have hit us hard and probably done a lot more damage.

*　　*　　*

Aeroperu left about on time, 6 PM, and arrived in Lima on time, about 10 PM. However, the 11 PM departure for Miami did not leave until 2 AM. So far on the trip Aeroperu was on time four times and late four.

Altogether, the tour was pretty good. Tara Tours could not be held liable for Aeroperu's failure to keep its schedule but it might be blamed for using Aeroperu at all. Our travel agent was a wealth of misinformation and bad planning. She scheduled us on Aeroperu, missed the market day in Cuzco and sent us to Peru during the national election and to Buenos Aires over a national holiday. We missed tours of Lima and Iquitos. We were there for a bomb blast in Cuzco, lots of guns in Peru, theft of my electric razor and a car wreck in Buenos Aires. But the weather was reasonable, there were no major health or language problems. We, also, shot a lot of film and video tape and experienced a lot to talk about.

*　　*　　*

20-23 June. Lima to Miami to Orlando and San Antonio

The plane got off at 0200 for Miami. We flew for a long time around weather with lightening ripping the sky over Colombia. The sky began to lighten with the false dawn while we were over *Lake Maracaibo* and the *Gulf of Venezuela*. The *Paraguano Peninsula* with the islands of Aruba and Curacao was back-lighted and stood out ghost-like against the dark sea.

Another half hour the yellow-orange band of brightness expanded and contracted between the red, bottom-lighted clouds and the dark sea. The sky shifted from a dark gray to a pale green, then to a nothing color that became a light blue as a bright golden sun peeked over the horizon. The yellow band shrunk and lavender bands of clouds crossed an expanding light blue band that pushed away the night. Mountains appeared dark against dark gray sea as we passed over the Dominican Republic and Haiti.

Early daylight cast shadows of cirrus clouds on the cottony stratus clouds below that hid Puerto Rico. Mountainous cumulus morning thunderheads penetrated the stratus layer marking the shallow water and island masses of the Bahamas Island chain. We were still at altitude with an almost black sky as Exuma Island and the Tongue of the Ocean Island came into view. Andros Island, with its pine forest, was visible from a much lower flight level. We passed to the south of Bimini and straight west into Miami International Airport, about two hours late.

*   *   *

Customs and immigration were no problem. Being late, we missed the United flight to Orlando and had to wait two hours for a US Air flight. We arrived in Orlando a little after lunch. Carol checked out a car while I rounded up the luggage. In short order, we were off for the motel at Disney World.

The next morning we were up early and arrived at the Epcot Center as it opened and spent the day and more, until 11 PM, in Tomorrowland. There were a lot of people but there was no sensation of being crowded. With jet lag and sensory overload, not much was memorable in Tomorrowland. We had lunch in a German beer hall and supper in a Norse castle.

The next morning, we took the Disney studio tour. The only really memorable ride was one built like a flight simulator. That, the Temple of Doom demonstration set and the good weather were the highlights. Carol dozed through the canons firing in the Temple of Doom program and by noon she was ready to go home.

We still had Saturday morning and a pair of Disney tickets. It was raining so instead of Disney World, we hit a big discount mall on the way to the airport in the rain.

It was 1100 and, again, United wasn't ready when we were. After about an hour overdue, they announced that the plane had not left Palm Beach because of mechanical problems. About three hours later the flight was cancelled. Those going to Los Angeles were rerouted and a special plane was sent to take all the Houston passengers to Houston. We left Orlando for Houston about the time we were supposed to arrive in San Antonio.

There was a two hour layover in Houston so I called Dr Harry and discussed the trip. We finally arrived in San Antonio about 7 PM.

*   *   *

Afterthoughts

After a trip is over is the time to reflect on the trip, things to do different and things to forget before the trip becomes dulled with time.

One thing we probably will not do again is take a trip where half the time is spent orbiting around airports and airplanes. Tension, boredom, discomfort, irregular meals and lack of good sleep are some of the disadvantages. The limited time someplace is divided between the desire to see everything and the urge to rest, sleep, take a hot shower and change clothes, eat a good meal—the reasons for taking a vacation are at odds with survival.

If we use a tour agent again it will be one that has time for clients and is not out to luncheons or business meetings all the time. We might get a call back in a few days and no one else in the office had any information on our questions.

Instead of a tour we will probably book passage and hotels and take local tours rather than packages that are rushed.

All future trips will be planned and scheduled by us. I may never take a packaged tour again except for day trips. The trip planner should know the area to be visited through research. The planner should check on weather, holidays, transportation, legal requirements, and activities available. The trip should be planned in a flexible way that will adapt to unexpected occurrences.

Been there. Done that.

Birds/Herps/Fish of South America

Herps
tree frog	MachuPichu
red and black lizard	Amazon
dead leaf toad	Amazon

Fish
red piranha (Serrasalmo rhombeus)	Amazon
sharp-nosed piranha group Pygocentrus piraya	Amazon

Birds
Least Terns(Sterna albifrons),	Machu Pichu
small sparrow-like birds	Machu Pichu
Mountain Wren (Troglodytes solstitalis)	Machu Pichu
Greater Ani (Crotophaga major)	Iquitos/Amazon
White-capped Flycatcher	Iquitos
Black Vultures (Coragyps aratus)	Iquitos
Turkey Vulture (Cathartes aura)	Amazon
Green Oropendola (Psarocolius viridis)	Amazon
Yellow-Headed Parrots (Amazona ochrocephala)	Amazon
Scarlet Macaw (Ara macao)	Amazon
Wattled Jacanas (Jacana jacana)	Amazon
Yellow-backed Oriole (Icterus chrysater)	Amazon
Black-Collared Hawk (Busarellus nigricollis)	Amazon
Gray Hawk (Buteo nitidus)	Amazon
Ring-billed Kingfishers (Ceryle torquata)	Amazon
Gray-capped Flycatcher (Myiozetetes grandensis)	Amazon
Black-tailed Flycatcher (Myiobus articaudus)	Amazon
Hermit Hummingbird (Phaethornis sp.)	Amazon
Toucanette (Aulacorhynchus sulcatus)	Amazon
Oven Bird (Seiurus aurocapillus)	Amazon
Horned Screamers (Anhima cornuta)	Amazon

Greater Potoo (<u>Nyctibius grandis</u>)   Amazon

Animals

Spider monkey	Amazon
Marmoset	Amazon
Pink Dolphin	Amazon

Trees and plants

Eucalyptus trees	Lima and Cuzco
Trees they locally called "Retama" planted on the medians	Cuzco
A grass from Kenya	Cuzco
dandelions	Cuzco and MachuPichu
pepperweed	Cuzco
Cerus peruvianas	Valley to Machu Pichu *Puya*
red bromeliads, <u>Puya alpestris</u>,	Near Machu Pichu
Peach trees	MachuPichu
strawberries	MachuPichu
several native beans	MachuPichu
mosses	MachuPichu
liverworts	MachuPichu
lichens	MachuPichu
ferns like Boston fern	MachuPichu
Venus flytrap plants, <u>Dionaea sp</u>.	MachuPichu
Gladiolas (introduced)	MachuPichu
Begonia Begonias (<u>B</u>. <u>coccinea</u>?)	MachuPichu
The potato, <u>Solanum tuberosum</u>	MachuPichu
<u>Solanum</u>, <u>S</u>. <u>muricatum</u> called *Pepino*	MachuPichu

small yellow mallows	MachuPichu
small yellow composites	MachuPichu
<u>Pentstemmon</u>	MachuPichu
<u>Calceolarius</u>	MachuPichu
<u>Fuchsia magellanica</u>	MachuPichu
several orchids	MachuPichu
<u>Lapageria</u> <u>sp</u>. or a large cigarette flower	MachuPichu
<u>Hydrocotyle</u>	MachuPichu
Three species of Oxalis (probably *O*. <u>carnosa</u>,	MachuPichu
<u>O</u>. <u>hedysaroides</u>	MachuPichu
<u>O</u>. <u>herrerae</u>)	MachuPichu
Clover (?)	MachuPichu
sow thistle (?)	MachuPichu
Acanthaceae—shrimp plant (<u>Belopherone</u> <u>sp</u>.)	MachuPichu
Coffee berries(Coffea sp.)	MachuPichu
ferns similar to Bracken (<u>Pteridium</u> <u>sp</u>.)	MachuPichu.
delicate evening primrose	
with perfect half-inch pink flowers.	MachuPichu
A vine with four inch long heart-shaped leaves sprouted	
two-inch purple flowers.	MachuPichu
Red Indian Paint Brush (<u>Castilleja</u> <u>sp</u>.)	MachuPichu
Kapok (<u>Ceiba</u> <u>pentandra</u>)	MachuPichu
Bread fruit (<u>Artocarpus</u> <u>atilis</u>)	MachuPichu
Pummello (<u>Citrus</u> <u>grandis</u>)	MachuPichu
Papaya (<u>Carica</u> <u>Papaya</u>)	MachuPichu
African Tulip tree (<u>Spathodea</u> <u>campanulata</u>)	Iquitos/Amazon
Manilla and other palms	Iquitos/Amazon
Red Hibiscus (<u>Hibiscus</u> <u>rosa-sinensis</u>)	Iquitos
Bananas (<u>Musa</u> <u>spp</u>)	Iquitos/Amazon
Taro (<u>Colocasia</u> <u>esculenta</u>)	Iquitos/Amazon
Cecropia tree (<u>Cecropia</u> <u>sp</u>).	Amazon
red kapok (<u>Ceiba</u> <u>pentandra</u>)	Amazon

Nipa Palm(<u>Nipa</u> <u>fruticans</u>)	Amazon
Swordgrass	Amazon
Brazil- or Para-nut tree (<u>Berthollrtia</u> <u>excelsa</u>)	Amazon
Acai (<u>Euterpe</u> <u>oleracea</u>)	Amazon
Pau-Brazil (<u>Caesalpinia</u> <u>echinata</u>)	Amazon

See the world while you can. See the best parts twice.
I'd like to see the Amazon in the wet season someday.

Carl